The "Big Questions" of Life

One man's lifetime search
for Big Answers

ERIC TEGELBERG

WESTBOW
P R E S S®
A DIVISION OF THOMAS NELSON
& ZONDERVAN

WestBow Press books may be ordered through booksellers or by contacting:

WestBow Press
A Division of Thomas Nelson & Zondervan
1663 Liberty Drive
Bloomington, IN 47403
www.westbowpress.com
844-714-3454

ISBN: 978-1-6642-6289-8 (sc)
ISBN: 978-1-6642-6288-1 (e)

Library of Congress Control Number: 2022906586

Print information available on the last page.

WestBow Press rev. date: 06/29/2022

This book is dedicated to my immediate family and to anyone who is thinking about the puzzling questions in life.

I want to thank Laurie Gillespie & George Jackson for their diligence in reviewing my manuscript and their helpful ideas.

I want to thank Pastor Jerry Rueb, Pastor Steve Bryant, Bob & Ann Paul and Michael Green all who first opened up the scriptures to me in a way that shone the eternal light into my life.

<u>Boundary Bay Dike</u>
<u>Why Did I author this Book?</u>

FOREWORD

Someone asked me two questions when I talked about this book on which I was working. The first question they asked was "What makes you think these questions are the Ten Biggest Questions of Life?" My answer to him was that they are the most important questions because they go to the central purpose of "Why am I here?" When you examine the many alternate questions like:

"Who should I marry?"
"What work should I do?"
"Am I being effective in my life?"
"How will I know what to do?"
"What school should I go to?"

Each of these are secondary to the reason of why I am here. The starting point of that question is "Does God Exist." This is the start point, because if God exists then there are significant contingencies and accountabilities for all of life. If God does not exist, then everything is without purpose and ultimately pointless. "Drink & be merry for tomorrow we die."

If that is so, then to live as a true atheist or a true materialist leads to a life exempt from morals, that is destined for oblivion. Now some people think that would be good because I could do whatever I want. I want to live free without the constraints of "laws and morals". However, you will fall into the hands of "might is right" crowd and that is not a world order that bodes well for the masses. As such, why would anyone want to continue to live life, as there is no purpose. Why would you have children if we all are destined for oblivion.

There is also one basic flaw in humanity with which everyone of us needs to come to grip - Death. This fact is evident that the outcome is one per person. Death being irrevocable makes these "Big Questions" <u>Urgent</u> and <u>Pressing</u> for each of us, regardless of how much we procrastinate. I invite you to write out your own thoughts on my answers to the Ten Great Questions of Life. If God exists which I believe He must exist, then He has an effect on each of these questions.

The second question they asked me was "why you?" What makes you think you might have the answer to these questions? I have had a trust in God from an early age, but I spent my years at university examining many of these ideas then drifted along getting my business and personal life underway. It was not until I was forty that I began the research to validate the truth to decide for myself what the answers to these questions must be. I am now over seventy so I have had a long time to consider these questions.

I have also investigated all the main line religions of the world, to see how they approach these ten questions. I have chosen to tackle each question from the point of view of the Judeo-Christian viewpoint, versus the atheist viewpoint. In an attached Addendum I deal with most of the ten Questions based on the eastern world religions. For answers to their approach visit Addendum 1, 2 & 3.

Boundary Bay Coast, Delta Canada

CONTENTS

PART 1

Does God Exist?

The starting point of each of these questions must be "Does God Exist." I have done a lot of reading on both sides of this question. After a lot of thought and research on this question I have concluded that God does exist. There are several factual propositions that lead me to this conclusion:

+ The Cosmos starting by chance, is unworkable!
+ Nothing caused the cosmos, is a violation of the law of causality!
+ If the cosmos had a beginning, it cannot be infinite.
+ The fine tuning of the universe speaks to an intelligent designer.
+ Human DNA is a programing language of men & beasts that speaks of a designer.
+ The cross-cultural idea of human morality demands a law giver.

The starting point of each of these "Big Questions" is "Does God exists? If He does, then there are significant contingencies for all of life. If God does not exist, then everything is without purpose. If you do not know where you are going then any road will get you there. However, I think there is more than enough evidence to convince every thinking person that God does exist.

Is there a God of order and magnitude that exceeds all we know in this world?

The universe is governed by laws and has such mathematical precision that it can only point to a personal designer and creator, who has left imprints of His supernatural existence. He has created man as a significant pinnacle in the created order. Our DNA, our intellect, our self-awareness and existential thought, all point to the fact that there is a designer of the cosmos as well as of the laws of physics and the constants that appear in the cosmos. Let us look now at some of the objections to this idea and the results of significant research into those listed above.

A. The Cosmos is started & created by Chance!

The Starting point of everything then is who made man and the cosmos. It may be that you think that it is "All Chance" but that answer is a copout. Here is why. Normally "Chance" is defined by "possibility, probability or happening which can be predicted." When you define the chance that a coin will turn up heads or that two dice will turn up seven, they are dependent or defined by the coins or dies' design AND the person casting them out. So, if you say that the beginning of the cosmos and man was chance, your logic is circular. In order for, "chance" to be the origin of everything, then there must be an intelligent existence that is both the source and concept of matter and energy. That is unless you think that all this cosmos is just an illusion as some eastern religions profess. Chance must be dependent upon a designer who is both the "builder" of the cosmos and the "originator of the design" of the event of the cosmos, for it to exist.

Those who are afraid to accept the possibility of a designer would rather define "Chance" as "the absence of any cause of events that can be predicted, understood or controlled." They are then stating that…"no thing caused it".

B. <u>Nothing Caused the Cosmos?</u>

So where are we with the beginning of everything? Some say that the cosmos came from nothing. Something that comes from nothing is contradiction of the "Law of Causality" which states that:

"Every effect must have a (necessary) cause greater than its effect to exist".

So, for the cosmos to exists, it must have an "uncaused first cause" which is greater than what we know exists today. In searching for that uncaused first cause, we again arrive at the necessary uncaused first cause who by necessity must be greater than what we know as the cosmos. We look to that first causal agent who is outside of time, matter and space AND whose knowledge & abilities must be beyond our comprehension and full understanding. This cause cannot be naturally created but must be a supernatural cause. So, if the cosmos exists as we know it does in "time" and "space", then there must be an uncaused <u>first-cause who is supernatural</u> who we identify as God who transcends time, matter & space and whose knowledge character and abilities are beyond us.

C. <u>If the Cosmos is Infinite; then it may be without Cause?</u>

If the cosmos was infinite, then it too would be outside time & space. However, Edwin Hubble showed that the cosmos is expanding at a defined rate. Therefore, we have evidence of a start which is known as "the Big Bang Theory" of cosmology. The uncomfortable conclusion of scientists today, is that;

"If there was beginning then there <u>had</u> to be a cause."

Physicists John Barrow & Frank Tipler observe about the moment of the big bang, "At this singularity, space and time came into existence; literally nothing existed before the singularity, so, if the universe originated at such a singularity, we would truly have a creation out of nothing." However, they postulate a cause that does not meet the Law of Causality.

There are others who say, "well this may be one of many universes in an infinitude of Cosmos." This too is trying to slip out of the Gordian knot of acknowledgement that there is a need for a first cause greater than the effect (one Cosmos or multiple cosmos). We know at least for this one Cosmos; we have evidence that it started at a point in time (i.e., time zero+). If it had a start, it needed a cause greater than itself, that is outside time, space & matter.

D. Fine Tuning of the Universe:

Science has determined that there are several measured values which reveal a universe that is finely tuned to an exacting degree. The "Laws of Physics" which are measurable are just too precise for anyone to maintain that the cosmos is caused by chance or blind happenstance. A list compiled by Victor Weisskopf for American Scientist (65,1977; 405) put forth the following list:

1. *Unification of Celestial & Terrestrial Mechanics: the same laws of nature hold throughout the universe.*
2. *Existence of Atomic Species: All matter is a result of combining around a hundred different kinds of atoms.*
3. *Heat as Random Motion: Heat is due to motion of material particles and is not a substance.*
4. *Unification of Electricity, Magnetism and Optics: All these are manifestations of electromagnetic fields.*
5. *Evolution of Living Species: Life & Biological complexity arose as described neo-Darwinian synthesis.**
6. *Relativity Theory: Space & time are unified into four-dimensional space-time; whose curvature corresponds to gravitational fields.*
7. *Quantum Theory: There are limits on the subatomic level to classical motions like position & momentum due to the causal indeterminacy.*
8. *Molecular Biology: the discovery of the DNA macro-molecule revealed the genetic code responsible for the development of living species.*
9. *Quantum "Ladder": Material systems are hierarchically ordered such that the smaller the system the greater the energy packed into it, thus unlocking the secret of nuclear energy.*

10. *Expanding Universe: the universe has an evolutionary history that began in the Big Bang.*

I list these to point out that there is widespread agreement that the universe is remarkably fine-tuned in terms of the laws of physics, all of which must line up in exacting proportion or there could be no sun or earth nor could there ever be life on earth. What does that mean to us when we have not made a life's work in studying any one of these fields?

This points to the probability that our one universe, which works so precisely can exist only as a function of chance. That chance has been calculated to be in the order of magnitude of having every roulette wheel on earth spinning and producing the number 27, at the same time and on the same day several times in a row. We on earth and in this cosmos have won that lottery of life because we know we exist. However, to have come to that winning place took immense fine tuning that speaks to a designer whose intelligence and power is unfathomable by human standards. Furthermore, it speaks to a designer who is personal and concerned with the beings on earth because he planned and created a cosmos that was specifically designed to support life on earth.

E. Fine Tuning of Human DNA:

One of the reasons that I included the above Weisskopf list, was because it shows intellectual bias of scientists who insist they know the truth. They believe that Christians do not have anything but faith. However, Item 5 is an anomaly in the list "described neo-Darwinian synthesis". This is something that they accept on faith without proof of science.

Let us look at DNA. Deoxyribonucleic acid (DNA) is of such determinative complexity that it runs counter to the tenants of macro-Darwinian Theory. DNA does connect with micro-evolution such as dog or horse breeding but for the determination of species it is bankrupt. DNA is a FOUR-character language, which is the determinative of species.

You might be able to get 100 monkeys typing on computers to produce one page of a Shakespearean sonnet. However, you cannot do that without autocorrect programmed into the monkeys' computer designed in Japan

& America by engineers and built in China by factory workers. DNA is a programming language which is far more complex than binary language used in a computer. Only a small subset of humanity is unlocking this knowledge-based language today. Its complexity is taking many researchers years to determine what value each part of the molecule has; what causes each character to change and the effects each character has on all living things.

No one I have ever heard of yet has asked Ancestry.com for an answer as to their ancestors. Then got the answer:

> "That your mother's people were Neanderthals & your grandparents on your father's side were Great Apes from southern Africa."

Why is that? Because DNA precludes that answer! DNA is specific to each Specie.

DNA is a complex configured cellular component of four alternating deoxyribose and phosphate molecules structured as a helix with specific nitrogen bases which determine specific messages within cells and between cells that determine specie, genetics, gender and reproduction specifics. It has been described as able to carry specific and complex messaging to the operation of each cell that if it were collected from humans it would be the equivalent to one thousand sets of Encyclopedia Britannica. Furthermore, as we see on the multiple "CSI" themed programs on television as well in many mystery novels, DNA is specific to each person as well as each specie. Whether you leave behind a hair, spittle or fingernail, a scientist can determine who was there because your specific DNA is in all of your cellular makeup.

This speaks to a specific complexity in humans and all organic species which requires a Designer who is designing each being with a specific purpose and environment in mind. This also speaks to a Designer who is planning for the future of man and beast. The design in that DNA is written how you will reproduce and prosper on earth, in every environment that is foreseen in that design. This speaks to the fact that the designer has taken a personal interest in specifying who you or any other being will adapt to their environment with care and purpose for each specie.

F. __Human Morality:__

There is one other item that points to God's existence being a true fact. The very notion of so-called "law and order" points to an over-arching social order. There is law in the world of man. Much of it invented by men and practiced by lawyers. Laws come from our sense of right and wrong which we call "morality". There is a cross cultural morality that clearly exists. It is absolute in human nature and you do not have to go far to determine it.

- ✧ Just step into the front of a line to see the reaction you get from those who have been waiting.
- ✧ Just grab a stranger & threaten them with a weapon and see where you end up.
- ✧ Just walk into a yard in full view of your neighbor and begin to dig out their flowers & trees for your own yard to see what happens.

These are all behaviors that we as a society find unacceptable. These behaviors are also cross cultural. One reason we are rejecting authority figures, media and organizations is because they are being discovered to perpetrate 'untruths'. This undermines our trust which breaks down our "faith" in them. Faith and trust are directly connected though the moral under-pinning's of every culture.

Where does this morality come from? Some of it is in laws passed down by society. However, there is a "meta-narrative" that goes beyond the legal system and has existed for thousands of years. You do not have to teach a two-year-old in any culture, that when someone steals your penguin, you want it back. Not now, but right now! Furthermore, he will hold those who took it or who were party to the theft accountable for months on end. This is indicative of an absolute morality that comes naturally to the two-year-old regardless of how much you teach them about "sharing". They understand the difference between sharing and theft.

Now you may say "but laws that are passed are all we need". "They are relative to the society's values". All you need to look at is the trouble people get in when they try to define what is "American" or "Canadian" values. Furthermore, when we look back in recent history to find what is <u>relative morality</u>, as defined in Germany, Russia or China, which led to wide-scale genocide the idea of cultural norms being defined by governments lacks trust. It has significant and sizable historical malfeasance. So, there is a clear difference between morality which is absolute and crosses cultural lines and "situational morality" which is found in groups and can change over time. "Absolute Morality" requires an Absolute Lawgiver. The absolute "Law Giver" must be outside humanity to be able to both legislate true absolute morality and to enforce it. There is only "One" such law giver. It can only be God.

Furthermore, there is within ever human evidence of a conscience that directs and also formulates guilt. This conscience is evidence of the Absolute Morality in each person. In fact, until recently if you demonstrated that you did not exhibit a conscience, you would have been treated for mental illness. However, as the society loses it conscience, by defining behaviors that were immoral to be now considered acceptable, we see more and more disillusionment with society. Maybe because it is becoming more removed from true Morality. It is easy to blame authorities and influencers in society but when you oppose your own conscience trouble is your destination.

G. <u>Conclusion:</u>

My conclusion is based on solid logic and truth found in these Six facts. They all point to the irrevocable conclusion that there must be a designer of life and of the Cosmos.

- ✦ <u>The Cosmos had a start, therefore must have a cause.</u>
- ✦ <u>Out of Nothing, nothing can come that is sufficient to cause the Cosmos.</u>
- ✦ <u>The Cosmos is finite which needs a cause outside of time space and matter.</u>
- ✦ <u>The Fine Tuning of the Universe points strongly to a designer.</u>

+ The intricate language of Human DNA points to a programmer, designer.
+ Human Morality points to a Law giver.

The logical answer that is based on these six well attested to facts, leads us to see the necessity for a creator to exist. If there is such a being, when I talk about faith, you need to place that word in the context of the six overwhelming significant realities that are listed above. Faith is trust based in sound reasoning, not just wishful thinking. Faith based on solid reason leads to Hope. That hope will get you through life. Without hope as Richard Dawkins put it:

> "In a universe of electrons and selfish genes, blind physical forces and genetic replication, some people are going to get hurt, and other people are going to get lucky; and you won't find rhyme or reason to it, nor any justice. The universe that we observe has precisely the properties we should expect if there is, at the bottom, no design, no purpose, no evil, no good, nothing but pitiless indifference" (River Out of Eden; NY: Basic Books, 1996; 133)

In Richard Dawkins world, there can be no God; regardless of the evidence, because he will only consider matter. Dawkins is captive to a monochrome view of a Kodachrome Cosmos. He denies the supernatural, even with the evidence that faces him. In my view the supernatural is both possible and probable. More specifically, it is required.

However, I would direct us to the second great question that we need to answer, before we tackle the question of "Is there life after death"! That question is "If God exists, which we see that He must, then has He revealed Himself to us?" I would answer with three proofs that He has revealed Himself.

+ The first is the speech of "general revelation" of nature. His authority and personality are revealed in the intricacies of the cosmos and worldly creation "Nature" works with design and mathematical precision.

+ The second proof is the universal evidence of a moral order or over-arching laws that we can see in the way all communities operate. Ideas such as prohibitions against "stealing, murder and lying" are universally accepted.

+ The universal acceptance that the family unit is accepted as the foundational building blocks of all civilization. When we try to circumvent these, we know that chaos will ensue. These have been demonstrated throughout the history of humanity.

Interestingly the third proof is in a compilation of writings of people who have had a relationship with this "Being" over the history of humanity. This is recorded for us in the collection of ancient writings that are written in three different languages by forty different writers over 1600 years of history. These writers when you examine their testimony are remarkably consistent in revealing what God is like and what he expects of us.

PART 2

Has God Said Anything?

Let me first tackle the issue of other religions. Both Islam and Judaism make claims to having the word of God as their foundation. Christians believe they too have the word of God as their foundation with the Old Testament from Judaism and the New Testament of Christianity. So, the question for each of these is tell me why yours is "the book" through which God has spoken. I will return to Islam at the end.

Can there be more than one account of God Speaking:

A. Yes, there can be more than one account of God Speaking!

If God is a personal God who is interested in relationship with His creation, then yes, He is going to speak to many people down through the ages. However, He will always be consistent with His message and will not err in anything He says. He will not contradict Himself over time nor will he make logical errors in what He says. He does these things because He is God who is loving, immutable (unchanging) and all knowing. Furthermore, the Jews view of God as derived from the Old Testament is the same God represented in the New Testament. The difference being that the Jews recognize Jesus of Nazareth as a prophet & great teacher

(Rabbi). They refuse to accept Jesus as the Son of God nor the Messiah that was prophesied to come. Therefore, they reject the New Testament.

B. <u>How can we identify the Record of God Speaking?</u>

> First, the transmission of God's word must be reliable down through time.
> Second, there must be physical evidence against which historical facts spoken about can be verified.
> Third, prophetic statements about future events must be verifiable as occurring, as foretold.
> Fourth there must be internal consistency within the scriptures, which has power to change lives.
> Fifth, when God who is Spirit and noncorporeal speaks there must be witnesses as to what was said, who record those words, and they must be transmitted faithfully down through further generations.

So, when we look at the Old Testament – the Jewish record of God speaking **AND** the New Testament of the Record of God and Jesus speaking, we find a collection that fits all the above criteria.

The 66 books of the Bible are a collection of forty different writers. These Books were written over a period of 1600 years and have an internal consistency within the 66 books. This is remarkable given the variable background of the writers:

> time of writing: First books are dated around 1500-1400BC thru to 90AD.
> Occupations of the writers: kings, priests, doctor, farmers, shepherd, fishermen & even a tax collector.
> Language written of the writers: Hebrew, Aramaic & (Koine) Greek.

The Record of God Speaks:

1. Transmission:

a) Manuscript Evidence:

There are currently in existence over 5,660 copies of manuscripts of the New Testament that date back as early as the second century. There are many papyrus segments that date back to within decades of the death of Christ. The most famous being John Rylands manuscript (P52) which is an excerpt of the Gospel of John. There are more than three hundred manuscripts described as Codex Sinaiticus and Codex Vaticanus that date to the fourth century. There are some twenty-eight hundred minuscules that date back to the ninth century. In total there are more than six thousand manuscripts in Greek. In addition to that there are more than ten thousand manuscripts in Latin. This does not count a substantial source in Slavic, Ethiopian and Armenian that all date before 1000AD.

Furthermore, the Old testament Hebrew and Greek record of the old testament is substantial. It is underwritten by the finding of the Dead Sea Scrolls in 1948. Within the find was a complete copy of the Book of Isaiah. When compared with the oldest known manuscripts of Isaiah, there were found to be 25 variants in the complete book. A variant is a different spelling of a word or a character variant in the written word. Not one of these variants would change the context or meaning in any substantial way.

One other significant piece of evidence for the security of transmission over time, is that in the writings of the first century and second century fathers (Justin Martyr, Irenaeus, Clement of Alexandria, Origen, Tertullian and others) it is estimated that there is enough quoted scripture from the New Testament to piece together the entire twenty-seven books from the New Testament, if all other sources were to be lost. The dates on those writers range from 90AD through to 195AD.

b) Textual Science:

What exists in the record of the old and new Testaments is a substantial record which Bible translators can use to determine, with absolute assurance, the original record that the autographic writers were writing. This is because of the science of textual criticism. The criticism that the Bible is a copy of a copy of a copy is without merit given the substantial record of ancient copies. There are copyist errors but they do not all make the same error. Therefore, the comparison between the older and newer copies will flesh out the true original writings. This provides a strong confidence that the autograph can be realized and known. Furthermore, by reading various translations from the original languages, your understanding as to what the original writers put down, as their books of the old and new testament becomes very trustworthy.

c) Textual Copyist:

At the time that the different books of the old and new Testaments were being originally written there were no printing presses. So, how were books printed? The answer to that is they were copied by hand, tediously, by a class of priests known as the "scribes". These people were set apart to reproduce scrolls and other manuscripts, which they considered holy books.

They went about their jobs in a methodical way. First, the "scribe" would speak the word out verbally, then they would write a letter of the word. Next, they would look back at the original word, then they would come back and write the next letter, then look again and so on until the word was complete. This would be done until the line was complete. Then a "sopher" (counter) would tally first the words, then letters for each line or column of the text and compare this to the original. This was a full-time occupation for priests who were classed as scribes and sophers. They began this process at the time of Moses and continue it to this day. Why would they do this in such an exacting methodical way? It is because their whole life was tied to the preservation of the Holy Scriptures. The Scriptures that the nation of Israel held in exalted status.

So, when critics suggest that copyists were cavalier about their tasks, they badly misjudge the process (either out of ignorance or out of malice). There can be side notes in different copies that the copyists made, but the original texts were transmitted with care and verification. The side notes were often comments made about interpretations or commentaries about the events recorded. Many Bibles today have similar notations in the margins or bottom of the page with a numerical reference. No biblical scholar takes those notes to be part of the original text.

2. <u>Physical Evidence:</u>

The Books of the Bible writers wrote a record of specific people who existed in the time of their writing. The names of kings, priests and governors are all specific to the times, places and events that they recorded. In every case there are within the record, items and events that often are unflattering to the people involved. According to the old adage "history is written by the victors." However, that is not what you find in the books of the Bible. Kings are described as good or bad according to the way they governed and how they related to their God. Victories and defeats appear within the record in unvarnished form. Specific behaviors of people noted are not glossed over.

a) **Kings, Governors & Priests:**

From Old & New Testament times, the archeologists have found records of King David, King Omri, Governor Pontius Pilot and high priests "Caiaphas" and "Annas" who were chief priests during Jesus' time. There are also records of Jesus and John the Baptist in the writings of Flavius Josephus, Gaius Cornelius Tacitus, Gaius Suetonius Tranquillus and Plinius the younger. All of these wrote within sixty years of the three years of Jesus Christ's public mission on earth. Each of them substantiates Jesus performed miracles and was executed by Rome. Each also affirms that the tomb of Jesus was empty.

b) **Towns, Pools, Temples and Other Landmarks:**

The archeologists continue to uncover physical evidence that what is recorded in the bible is accurate. For example, in the Gospel of John, the writer in (John 2:11-13) correctly describes the changes in elevation between Cana in Galilee and Capernaum and Jerusalem in Judea. John also describes the difference between Bethany the home of Mary, Martha & Lazarus (John 11:18) as being two miles from Jerusalem and the Bethany beyond the Jordan River (John 1:28) more than 100 miles away. Only an ancient Palestinian (Israelite) would know these places.

Furthermore, John describes the Pool of Bethesda as surrounded by five colonnades (John 5:2) and the Pool of Siloam used by the infirmed (John 9:7). In June 2004, the Pool of Siloam was unearthed and it supported not only John's description but supported the fact the water supply for this pool was the very supply from the Gihon Spring, which is recorded in 2 kings 20, Isaiah 37 and 2 Chronicles 32:2-3. All of these are 500 years before Christ Jesus. This was the water supply that supported Jerusalem during the siege of the Assyrian King Sennacherib, in 701 BC. All of which are reported in the books cited above. This was confirmed in 1838 by Edward Robinson.

The pool of Bethesda was dismissed as foolishness because it had not been found and particularly it was the scene of the miracle healing of the paralytic. In 1956 this all changed when Drs. Timothy & Lydia McGrew excavated the pool based on John's description. It was found to be bounded by four colonnades with a fifth in the center just as John described. These are but two specific discoveries that have been made that verify the historical accuracy of the scriptures. There are literally thousands of finds that have appeared from digs and caves from Palestine (Israel) that add to the veracity of the events reported in scripture.

3. Prophetic statements are authenticated:

There are many prophetic statements made in scripture that stand out as only possible with knowledge that could not be human in origin. The history of Israel is foretold in very specific warning and promises. From the beginnings of Abraham and Sarah his wife, being called by God to leave his Chaldean home to go to a place God would give to him and his many offspring. to today where there are millions of Jews living in almost every country of the world. This proved the promises made to Abraham would be fulfilled, even though He only saw a glimpse of it in His own time.

a) Succession of Nations:

We find in the writing of the Book of Daniel (Daniel 2), a revealed vision of the dream that King Nebuchadnezzar, had one night, which distressed him greatly. The King called all the wisemen from his kingdom to come before him. He demanded that they tell him both, what his vision was and what it means. They all said to him we can only interpret what we know, but he refused to tell them His dream. Finally, Daniel, a captive from the destruction of Jerusalem by Nebuchadnezzar, volunteered to enlighten the King. Daniel was able to both to discern what the King had seen in his dream and to interpret what it meant.

The vision was of a great statue made of Gold on its head, silver in the upper body, bronze in the lower body, the legs made of iron and the feet made of iron and clay. The interpretation that is given, recorded in Daniel, is that there is to be a succession of kingdoms which will rule all of the known world from the head which represented Babylon, to the silver the Medes & Persian, then the Greeks under Alexander and finally Rome. All of whom were barely unknown or of little consequence at this time. Furthermore, there was the image of a hand which produced a great stone which was thrown at the feet crushing them which symbolized the coming of a kingdom which would establish itself during the last kingdom and would overpower the final kingdom. This represents the coming of Jesus Christ during the Roman era which would begin the growth of the world-wide church which would never end. Though the church of Christ would be persecuted from the First century of Caesars, through to the Third century in the coming of Constantine, the church of Christ would be given status within the Roman rule.

b) People and cities:

In Isaiah 44:24-45:1, there is a passage that predicts the restoration of Judah and Jerusalem after the captivity which is coming when Babylon invades and lays siege. There is a name given of a man who will appear on the scene some 80-100 later. His name is Cyrus. When he learns that even before he was born, God of the Jews had called him to defeat the Babylonians, He is surprised and chooses to set free the Israelites, taken into captivity by the Babylonians. King Cyrus is so astounded by this prediction that he does as God has predicted to the letter. He sets them free; the Jews return to Judah and rebuild Jerusalem and re-establish the Jewish temple.

What is even more astounding, the Prophet Jeremiah, after Isaiah's time, in Jeremiah 29:10, predicts that their captivity would last only 70 years. This correspond exactly to the time that the Babylonians ruled over their captivity and the date of the proclamation document being issued to release the Jews to return to Jerusalem and rebuild the city and the temple of God by Cyrus.

4. <u>Changed Lives:</u>

In the world there is plenty of evidence of changed lives of people who have come to believe and trust Christ. However, there are three in scripture that stand out for our purposes. These three stand out in the record because of who they are and how it is documented in the books of the New Testament. Furthermore, each one of these will encounter trials for their faith and writings. Ultimately, each one will be martyred for their faith.

Who would die for a lie that you knew was a lie? Now some would say this is another example of religious martyrdom that is based upon lies and distortions. Just as Muslims will do in bombing and personal attacks on non-believers for their faith, martyrdom is typical for religious fanatics. The difference is that these were killed by the religious authorities (the Sanhedrin or Roman Caesars') for speaking what they knew was the truth, because they were witnesses to it. The Muslim terrorist dies by self-destruction (suicide) on the promise that he will inherit a benefit in heaven. The terrorist dies for a lie at his own hand. The Christian martyr is killed for their witness statements of the truth and for refusing to recant those true witness statements.

a) Stephen the Martyr:

In the Book of Acts there is another uprising of the Jewish authorities against this new growing group of believers. In Jerusalem, the growth of the Christians is growing very rapidly with the start of roughly one hundred lead by the eleven Apostles to within weeks to more than six thousand. So, the Jewish rulers arrest a disciple named Stephan. Early in the Book of Acts, Luke the writer of Acts (Acts 6:1-7:58) describes the calling of seven men to act as deacons to handle the activities of feeding the widows and orphans in the Greek community of believers. Sometime later in Jerusalem, the Jewish authorities arrest Stephan. They bring him before their court (the Sanhedrin), with charges that Stephen is blaspheming God and speaking against the law of Moses. He testifies that he not speaking against Moses & the law but rather Moses testified about the coming of Jesus Christ. All that the laws and the prophets said about the coming Messiah fits Jesus of Nazareth. Then Steven accuses his accusers of not recognizing Jesus of Nazareth as being the prophet that Moses promised would come and that they were guilty of the wrongful murder of Jesus. The Sanhedrin then carries Steven out of the city and begin to stone him to death. He calls out to Jesus to forgive them because they do not realize what they are doing. This is the first Christian martyr on record, after the resurrection and ascension of Jesus. This man, Stephen, would rather die than deny his trust in Christ Jesus. Stephen trusted the words and promises of Jesus during His earthly ministry.

b) Paul the Persecutor:

The next witness with a changed life, was present at the stoning of Stephan. His name is Saul. The Book of Acts reports that Saul held the cloaks and coats of the stoning accusers. Saul becomes a persecutor of the early church of Christ, seizing people and delivering them to the Sanhedrin for judgment and death. In Acts 9, Saul goes to the High Priest to get arrest warrants for Jewish Christians in Damascus. As he is travelling there, Saul has a vision of the risen Christ,

> [3] *As he neared Damascus on his journey, suddenly a light from heaven flashed around him.* [4] *He fell to the ground and heard a voice say to him, "Saul, Saul, why do you persecute me?"*

> [5] *"Who are you, Lord?" Saul asked.*

"I am Jesus, whom you are persecuting," he replied. ⁶ "Now get up and go into the city, and you will be told what you must do." ⁽ᴺᴵⱽ⁾ (Acts 9:3-6)

Saul is struck blind and continues to Damascus. There he meets a Christian named Ananias, who Jesus has directed to go meet Saul and heal his blindness. Ananias does as directed, by the Holy Spirit, goes to Paul and prays for his healing. When healed, Saul becomes Paul, who will go on to write nearly two-thirds of what we know today as the New Testament. Saul the persecutor becomes Paul the Apostle, sent to the Gentile world to spread the good news of Jesus Christ. Paul too is martyred for his faith but never revokes his trust in Christ Jesus.

c) James the Brother:

Jesus had several brothers and sisters. We see them mentioned in the New Testament. During his earthly lifetime none of them believed that their brother Jesus, was who he said He was – the Son of God. In fact, it is recorded that the family members tried to get Jesus to stop preaching. However, when Jesus was crucified on good Friday, the only family member recorded to be present at the death of Jesus was His mother Mary. After His resurrection, Jesus appeared to many people. One of those was His brother James. James went on to be a leader in the early church and dies a martyr's death never having recanted his trust in his brother's claim to be the Son of God. James died fully expecting that Jesus would return to earth.

d) The Early Church of Christ:

The final witness of changed lives, comes from the early church, which was established in Jerusalem, largely from Jewish believers of Jesus Christ. Jews to this day celebrate Sabbath at sundown Friday night to sundown Saturday. According to 1 Corinthians 16:2 (56AD) and - Acts 20:7 (61-63AD), Christians were meeting on the first day of the week which would be Sunday. Given that the early church was largely converts from Judaism, why would they change their Sabbath date unless they had a life changing experience of witnessing the resurrected Jesus. They change the Sabbath day to recognize the day of the resurrection of Jesus and the discovery of the empty tomb. They changed the Sabbath because the resurrection proved that Jesus was the Son of God.

5. The witnesses of the documented words of God

The next group are witnesses of the sayings and actions of Jesus. They either write as original eyewitnesses or as recorders of eyewitness testimony of the accounts of Jesus sayings and actions.

a) John the Apostle:

John the Apostle wrote about what he heard and saw while walking with Jesus for the three years of Jesus' ministry in Palestine(Israel). His writings cover many teachings, incidents and miracles that he witnessed. John writes for an audience of new believers to emphasis the truth claims and divinity of Jesus. His book dates to within 40 years of the death of Christ Jesus. His book is the most theological of the four gospels. John believes and provides evidence of Jesus, described as "the Word of God" (John 1:1), "the Lamb of God" (John 1:29); the "Messiah" (John 1:41); "the Son of God" and "the King of Israel" (John 1:49). John calls Jesus "the Saviour of the world" (John 4:42); "the Lord ...and God" John 20:28). He also asserts Jesus' deity in a series of "I Am..." claims of Jesus (John 6:35; 8:12; 10:7, 9, 11&14; 11:25; 14:6; 15:1 & 5) that point to His being more than just a good man and sound teacher. Furthermore, John records Jesus making several I Am – (YHWH) the God of the Old Testament statements (John 4:24, 26; 8:24-28, 58-59; 13:18-19) which demonstrate Jesus' authority & power, that normal men could not have. Jesus reveals himself through yet another symbolic expression, "I am" (Gk. *ego eimi*). In the Greek Old Testament, the name of God revealed to Moses on Mount Sinai is *ego eimi*, or "I am" (Exod. 3:13f.)[1] The witness of John is controversial because he was reporting the statements of Jesus

---

[1] Burge, G. M. (1995). John. In *Evangelical Commentary on the Bible* (Vol. 3, p. 855). Grand Rapids, MI: Baker Book House.

that provoked the reaction of the authorities to put Jesus to death. They did that because they recognized what Jesus was saying. He admitted two things which enraged the authorities:

+ Being the "Son of God".
+ Being a greater prophet than Moses the Law Giver.

These statements are all made in connection with miracles that Jesus performed in his ministry and that Moses was credited as having done in the desert. We may see these statements as metaphors but the Jewish authorities saw them as authoritative and blasphemy.

b) Matthew the tax Collector:

The first book in the new Testament is written by a tax collector, Levi, who Jesus recruited to be a disciple early in the first year of His ministry. Being a Jew who collected taxes for the Roman authorities would not be a highly prized or trusted occupation as far as his fellow Palestinian (Israeli) citizens were concerned. However, if Levi/Matthew was a tax collector he would have to be literate in Hebrew, Aramaic and Konia Greek. Matthew's book dates to the early 60AD's and is less than 30 years from the date of Jesus death. Matthew writes to the Jewish audience and is concerned with the things that Jesus said and did that fulfilled Old Testament prophecy of the coming Messiah. The Book of Matthew is replete with references to Old Testament statements from the prophets. The other major theme of Matthew is that Jesus is the Son of David, making him the final and permanent King of Israel.

c) Luke the Doctor:

Luke was a first century physician and was a close friend of Paul, with whom he went on several missionary journeys. While Luke was not part of the original witnesses to Jesus' teaching, he had extensive contact with Peter, James and Mark, who were eyewitnesses, as well as Jesus' mother Mary and brothers and sisters. Luke's book was written to a Gentile audience. Luke states that In the opening of his account:

(Luke 1:1-3)

> *1:1 Many have undertaken to draw up an account of the things that have been fulfilled among us, 2 just as they were handed down to us by those who from the first were eyewitnesses and servants of the word. 3 Therefore, since I myself have carefully investigated everything from the beginning, it seemed good also to me to write an orderly account for you, most excellent Theophilus, 4 so that you may know the certainty of the things you have been taught.(NIV)*

Luke is the only record of the early life of Jesus. Luke and Matthew are the only records of the birth of Jesus and the genealogy of Jesus. The date of Luke was before the book of Acts which he also authored. Reliable estimates place Luke being written at 58-60AD and Acts at 61-63AD

d) Peter the Fisherman:

Peter wrote two letters that are part of the New Testament, 1 & 2 Peter. They are dated to 62-63 AD and 65-66AD. These letters were written in Rome before Peter was martyred by Nero in 67AD. Peter writes to emphasize the true doctrine of God's grace in the life of the believer and the assurance that Christ Jesus is the Lord of all and truly was raised from the dead. He counsels against heresies of false teachers. He encourages the church of Christ to endure the persecutions that are encountered and to live holy and submissive lives to the teaching of Christ. Peter dies a martyr's death at the hand of Roman authorities.

6. Witnesses to God speaking:

a) Mount Sinai:

In Exodus we find several witnesses to the audible voice of God speaking to specific people. The first is Moses who God called into service to lead the Israelites out of captivity (Exodus 3:4-4:17). Moses with his assistant Joshua records several conversations with God, which he records as the books of Genesis, Exodus, Leviticus and Deuteronomy. Once the tribes have been led out of Egypt, they appear before mount Sinai. (Exodus 19:3-24) At this moment, recorded in Exodus, thousands of Israelites hear the voice of God, all who cower in terror at this event. They receive the ten commandments and God covenantal promise to Israel.

b) Baptism of Jesus:

The Baptism of Jesus, by John the Baptist, is recorded in Matthew 3:13-17; Mark 1:9-11 and Luke 3:21-23. Each version records that God spoke audibly saying "This is (You are) my Son, whom I love with You I am well pleased." Each writer recounts this voice which was heard by many witnesses including John the Baptist and his disciples.

c) Transfiguration of Jesus:

A similar occurrence is recounted by Peter, James & John in Matthew 17:1-13; Mark 9:2-13 and Luke 9:28-36. This is on top of a mountain (Some believe it to be Mount Tabor at the eastern end of the Jezreel valley) where an audible voice is heard. They record statements saying, "This is my Son, whom I love (chosen)" and "With Him I am well pleased." "Listen to Him." These are witnessed by three of the disciples. Each one has similar descriptions of the event as recorded in Matthew & Mark. The descriptions are not exactly alike but have a veracity about them that you would expect from witness statements.

7. <u>Historical Reliability:</u>

One other remarkable feature of the Biblical writers is that they do not paint over the historical record of kings and figures in their written records. They tell of defeats, sins and offenses of kings and other historical people. Most records from courts of kings and governors try to put on a bold face for history. This is not the case of the Old and New Testaments. Cases in point are 1 & 2 Chronicles as well as Matthew & Luke in the new testament.

➢ **1 & 2 Kings**:

In the Books of Kings of Israel & Judah, there is a final assessment of each king as they serve and died. For example, we see a description the King of Israel, Baasha, at the time of Asa the King of Judah in 1 Kings 15 who ascends to the throne after his father Jeroboam dies.

1 Kings 15:33-34 Baasha King of Israel

33 In the third year of Asa king of Judah, Baasha son of Ahijah became king of all Israel in Tirzah, and he reigned twenty-four years. 34 He did evil in the eyes of the LORD, following the ways of Jeroboam and committing the same sin Jeroboam had caused Israel to commit. (NIV)

The assessment is not something that a King nor his press secretary would be allowing his historical scribe to record about him or his father. These assessments are common in the Books of 1 & 2nd Kings. They are there for all to see down through history.

➢ **Matthew & Luke**:

When it come to the New Testament records we see a similar record where the apostles are bickering and jockeying for position with Jesus for when He because King. In Matthew 20, we see the mother of the two sons of Zebedee comes to ask a favour of Jesus. She asks that they be granted to be His right & left hand (first & second ministers).

Matthew 20:20-27 A Mother's Request

20 Then the mother of the sons of Zebedee came up to him with her sons, and kneeling before him she asked him for something. 21 And he said to her, "What do you want?" She said to him, "Say that these two sons of mine are to sit, one at your right hand and one at your left, in your kingdom." 22 Jesus answered, "You do not know what you are asking. Are you able to drink the cup that I am to drink?" They said to

him, "We are able." ²³ He said to them, "You will drink my
cup, but to sit at my right hand and at my left is not mine to
grant, but it is for those for whom it has been prepared by my
Father." ²⁴ And when the ten heard it, they were indignant
at the two brothers. ²⁵ But Jesus called them to him and said,
"You know that the rulers of the Gentiles lord it over them,
and their great ones exercise authority over them. ²⁶ It shall
not be so among you. But whoever would be great among you
must be your servant, ²⁷ and whoever would be first among
you must be your slave, ²⁸ even as the Son of Man came not
to be served but to serve, and to give his life as a ransom for
many." (ESV)

Jesus corrects their scheming, with a very frank answer and a correction to their ideas of what serving in the Kingdom of God will be like.

In Luke, we see the report of Peter's denial of knowing Jesus on the evening of the six trials of Jesus before the authorities: Caiaphas, the Sanhedrin, Pilate and Herod. Peter would become one of the chief spokesmen for the formative church of Christ in Jerusalem does not try to edit out this account because like the assessments of the old testament records it was the truth.

Many are the historical records preserved by the "winners" that gloss over the truth for their position in history to be recounted unblemished. The records of the old testament and new testament writers report what happened whether it is embarrassing or favourable.

Conclusion:

One last thing that I should mention about what God has said to humanity: In John 14:22-26, when Jesus is talking to His disciples, He explain that He and the Father will send to them a "Counselor", a comforter who will be with them forever. "But the Counselor, the Holy Spirit whom the Father will send in my name, will teach you all things and will remind you of everything I have said to you." Here we have another reason to trust what is found in the Bible. As other writers have described in the Bible, the overseer who ensured that what is recorded and what is carried forward into time, is an accurate account of what God has said, is God Himself.

It is God through the Holy Spirit who oversees scripture transmission.

- ✧ Given that the books that make up the Bible have a historical context that places each one of them in or near time of the events they record, I find that they are a reliable and accurate account of the events they record.
- ✧ Given the physical evidence, which support the events they describe in surprising detail, I find the books of the Bible to be a valuable record of the times and places they describe.
- ✧ Given the prophetic statements found in the Bible about future people, events and nations, I find that the Bible is empowered by sources that are supernatural and astonishing in their accuracy.
- ✧ Given that the words and events recorded in the Bible have the power to change the lives of people who read, study and encounter the God of the Bible and His Son.
- ✧ Given that the Books of the New Testament are written by people who were there and speak as eyewitnesses or reproduced statements from eyewitnesses, then the Bible has authority of truth that is absolute in trustworthiness and veracity.
- ✧ Given that the Books of the Old and New Testament record specific people and people groups who heard God, in their context, then the Bible is significantly of a different origin than just stories of men. This lends credibility to the bible being inspired by a greater source than men.

I trust that those who engage the Holy Scriptures will not be put to shame nor will they die in vain. Furthermore, there is great encouragement and a warning given in the last lines of Revelation as a warning after the encouragement that there is great understanding to be gained by those who read it.

Revelation 1: 3 & 22:18-19

³ Blessed is the one who reads aloud the words of this prophecy, and blessed are those who hear it and take to heart what is written in it, because the time is near…(NIV)

¹⁸ I warn everyone who hears the words of the prophecy of this scroll: If anyone adds anything to them, God will add to that person the plagues described in this scroll. ¹⁹ And if anyone takes words away from this scroll of prophecy, God will take away from that person any share in the tree of life and in the Holy City, which are described in this scroll. (NIV)

PART 3

What must God be like?

When we consider What God must be like, there are really four ways we can go with this question.

- ➤ God is Spirit and takes a personal interest with all humanity and creation.
  - ○ This is the view of Judaism & Christianity.
- ➤ God is Spirit, but he is not personally involved with the world.
  - ○ This would be the view of Islam.
- ➤ God is a Spiritually consciousness apart from everything that exists. There is migration back to this consciousness to be incorporated into this Being upon death. We are the problem because we must eradicate self to attain indistinguishable existence with the spiritual consciousness that is universal.
  - ○ This is largely the view of the eastern religions. (Buddhism)
- ➤ God is a Universal Spirit. All in nature is God, there is no distinction between God and all that exists.
  - ○ This is largely the view of the Hinduism as well as many forms of animism or creature worship. (Sikhism, Jainism, Hinduism & Animism)

The view that makes most sense to me is the first view; that God is a Spirit who is personally involved with the world and in creation.

I will deal with other religions in a comparison of world religions later. Suffice it to say that for there to be a God who has created all things, it follows that there then needs to be a God who is all powerful (omnipotent), who sustains the creation daily. He must be eternal because without pre-existing before the beginning of time, there can be no beginning for all created things. He must be personal because he has revealed himself to all humanity:

❖ He has revealed Himself through His Creation, all that is existing in the Cosmos:

❖ He has revealed Himself with the Moral Law that is universally known.

❖ He has made Himself known by giving us His revelation in a collection of ancient writings we call the Bible.

> "*18 The wrath of God is being revealed from heaven against all the godlessness and wickedness of people, who suppress the truth by their wickedness, 19 since what may be known about God is plain to them, because God has made it plain to them. 20 For since the creation of the world God's invisible qualities—his eternal power and divine nature—have been clearly seen, being understood from what has been made, so that people are without excuse." (Romans 1:18-20)*

There exists, several writings from antiquity that make representation that they are the Words of God. Earlier on I made the defense as to why I accept the Bible as the stand-alone source of the revelation of this all-powerful God. Therefore, allow me to bring definition of "What is God Like", as revealed in and through the words of several different writers dating back to between 1600BC to 70AD. In the scriptures, God reveals several attributes that are called Incommunicable attributes and several Communicable attributes. The distinction here is, that a communicable attribute can be transferred and represented in and through others, while Incommunicable attributes cannot be transferred nor represented in others but exists in Himself alone.

In Psalm 9:10, King David, the writer, says of God that "Those who know your name trust in you, for you, Lord have never forsaken those who seek you." God is trustworthy for those who earnestly seek Him. To the true seekers of God, He will reveal Himself. He does that though the words that He has prompted other seekers to write. He will reveal Himself through the word of His Son, Jesus. He reveals himself through the guidance of the Holy Spirit whom He send to enlighten true seeker.

➤ Incommunicable Attributes:

I. God is Self-Existent (Aseity):

➤ "I AM WHO I Am" (Exodus 3:14, God speaks to Moses and tells him His name which is also an explanation of His being)

➤ Life in Himself (John 5:26, Both the Father & the Son)

> (John 5:26)"**26** For as the Father has life in himself, so he has granted the Son also to have life in himself.(NIV)

➤ First & the Last; The Alpha & Omega: The Beginning & the End; As the Beginning, God has no cause. (Isaiah 41:4; 44:6; 48:12; Revelation 1:8, 18; 2:8; 3:14; 21:6; 22:13)

Isaiah 44:6

> "**6** "This is what the LORD says—Israel's King and redeemer, the LORD Almighty: I am the first and I am the last; apart from me there is no God."(NIV)

When we consider the self-existence of God we are talking about the concept of immensity of God. God is outside of all things that exist. He has created immense things like the universe and tiny things like a single cell. Yet in a sense god contains them all, God oversees them all and He has contact with them all. We are told in scripture that when a sparrow fall that God is aware of its passing and He knows the number of hairs on your head. In the same sense He has placed every star in the universe and has named them all. So, from these we begin to see and appreciate that God has immensity that is effective in personally being connected to all points and things that exist.

Furthermore, God is the beginning and end of everything. His being is unconditional and not dependent on anything but Himself. Hence He is the great "I Am", controller and creator of everything. He is the only thing in existence that is unconditional. Humans are conditional in our existence is dependent first on conception and birth. Even after that our existence is dependent on our growth and learning to adulthood and beyond. God is not dependent on anyone and His immensity is effective on all things that exist.

➢ **Why is this important?** It is important in that God is not conditional, not derived nor is He dependent on anything. He is not a creature that was created. He has always existed. He will always exist. God is the sum of His attributes. All His attributes have always existed and can never:
  • be lost,
  • be increased,
  • be dependent on anything but Himself,
  • be dependent on circumstance.
  • So, God is never doing anything in order to meet a need or to satisfy an essential for Himself. Therefore, you can trust Him to be beyond reproach in all things that He does. You can trust Him to do and be as His character and personality dictate come whatever.

II. God is Transcendent:

➢ Separate from the World. (Isaiah 66:1-2; Acts 17:24)

> *(Isaiah 66:1-2)* *"⁶⁶:¹ This is what the* LORD *says: "Heaven is my throne, and the earth is my footstool. Where is the house you will build for me? Where will my resting place be? ² Has*

not my hand made all these things, and so they came into being?" declares the LORD. *"These are the ones I look on with favor: those who are humble and contrite in spirit, and who tremble at my word."* (NIV)

➢ Contrasted with the World. (Psalm 102:25-27; 1 John 2:15-17)

1 John 2:15-17

"15 Do not love the world or anything in the world. If anyone loves the world, love for the Father is not in them. 16 For everything in the world—the lust of the flesh, the lust of the eyes, and the pride of life—comes not from the Father but from the world. 17 The world and its desires pass away, but whoever does the will of God lives forever." (NIV)

God transcends all thing because he is outside of everything in that He is distinct from His creation. He affects His creation, but He is distinct from His creation. We, on the other hand, are affected by our connections. Our relationships to one another affect us daily. Our connection to the physical world around us affects us. In fact, in both of these, we are dependent for our health, our emotions and our development. God is transcendent and is only affected by His own will and His attributes.

God acts according to His attributes and His will. He will never act in contravention of his being. We can count on Him to be consistent when humans and our world around us are inconsistent and often unpredictable. God knows where history is being made and what were the causes and the affects. Transcendences means he can, at His will, see cause and effect before they occur and can choose to intercede or not, as His will determines.

➢ **Why is this important?** It is important in that God is entirely distinct, from what He has made. It gives Him independence and authority over His creation. God owns everything He has made. God transcends all laws of physics so in His transcendency, He can do whatever He wants: "Invent time", "do miracles" or "affect history". Being outside of time & matter, He is able to create without conditions, compatible with His character traits.

III. God is Immanent:

➤ God is near, so He can be known. (Deuteronomy 4:7; Jeremiah 23:23; Acts 17:27)

Jeremiah 23:23-24

> [23] *"Am I only a God nearby,"* declares the Lord, *"and not a God far away?* [24] *Who can hide in secret places so that I cannot see them?"* declares the Lord. *"Do not I fill heaven and earth?"* declares the Lord. (NIV)

➤ This is bound up with God's omnipresence. (Psalm 139:7-10; Jeremiah 23:24; Acts 17:28)

Deuteronomy 4:7,8

> [7] *For what great nation is there that has a god so near to it as the Lord our God is to us, whenever we call upon him?* [8] *And what great nation is there, that has statutes and rules so righteous as all this law that I set before you today?* (ESV)

The immanence of God is the recognition that He is near and substantially present everywhere. By the infinite power of God who is creator of all, He still is present to all He created. There is no point in the existence of the material or supernatural world that God is not present. By His immanence, He can affect and observes all that occurs. "God is omnipresent and immanent, penetrating everything even while He contains everything. The Bucket that is sunk into the depths of the ocean is full of the ocean. The ocean in in the bucket, but also the bucket is in the ocean – surrounded by it." (A.W. Tozer, 1997) This illustrates God's immanence. The creation is surrounded by the presence of God and the presence of God is existing around all the is creation. He does that in all of His fullness, without any reduction of His being.

➤ **Why is this important?** His being near to everything brings Him perfect knowledge of everything and He can affect everything perfectly as He chooses. He is a God who is near and not one who is distant from us. For the seeker of God, this is important in that he will reveal Himself to the seeker in many ways. To the one who is uninterested in knowing God, this means God is fully aware of who he is, what he does and how he lives. To both of these persons there is an assurance that when it comes to the judgement of God He has complete knowledge of everything that is that person, physically, spiritually, physical makeup and history.

IV. God is Omnipresent:

➤ The universe cannot contain God (1 Kings 8:27; Isaiah 66:1; Acts 7:48-49)

➤ Present everywhere equally. (Psalm 139:7-10; Acts 17:28) of Christ, (Matthew 18:20; 28:20)

> *(Psalm 139:7—12) "7 Where can I go from your Spirit? Where can I flee from your presence? 8 If I go up to the heavens, you are there; if I make my bed in the depths, you are there. 9 If I rise on the wings of the dawn, if I settle on the far side of the sea, 10 even there your hand will guide me, your right hand will hold me fast. 11 If I say, "Surely the darkness will hide me and the light become night around me," 12 even the darkness will not be dark to you; the night will shine like the day, for darkness is as light to you."(NIV)*

➤ Fills all things. (Jeremiah 23:23-24) of Christ, (Ephesians 1:23; 4:10; Colossian 3:11)

Acts 17:24-26

24 "The God who made the world and everything in it is the Lord of Heaven and earth and does not live in temples built by hands. 25 And He is not served by human hands, as if he needed anything. Rather, He himself gives life and breath and everything else. 26 From one man he made all the nations, that they should inhabit the whole earth; and he marked out their appointed time in history, and the boundaries of their lands."

By omnipresence, God is close to everything and everyone. When we see God, coming into the garden of Eden and asking Adam and Eve where they were, it was not because He didn't know where they were but that they were trying to hide from God. He is a God who is Omnipresent and is completely aware as to where they were hiding and what they had done.

So those who seek God can and will find Him because He is always near. God is not remote. He is personal and involved in all that there is in creation. Therefore, it is foolish to think God does not see or know, what we do and how we think. He has full knowledge because He is omnipresent.

➤ **Why is this important?** Again because of His presence everywhere He is able to ensure His will is done everywhere and all the time. Therefore, God is a perfect judge because He has witnessed every act on earth for all time and understands the heart motive of every individual.

V. God is Immutable:

➤ Unchangeable (Psalm 102:26-27; Isaiah 51:6; Malachi 3:6; Romans 1:23; Hebrews 1:11-12, 13:8; James 1:17)

   (Malachi 3:6) "6 "I the LORD do not change."(NIV)

➤ There are instances in scripture that seem to describe God changing his mind or relenting. They are always conditional upon the deeds of men. God does not change. He has no need to change knowing the past, the present & the future completely. (Ex. 32:9-14; Psalm 18:25-27.)

Psalm 18:25-27

25 To the faithful you show yourself faithful to the blameless you show yourself blameless, 26 to the pure you show yourself pure, but to the devious you show yourself shrewd. 27 You save the humble but bring low those whose eyes are haughty. (NIV)

Immutable is a word derived from Latin which means not subject to change. James writes that we are not to be deceived.

"Every good and perfect gift is from above, coming down from the Father of the heavenly lights, who does not change like the shifting shadows." (NIV)(James 1:17)

All things in creation are subject to change. We are not the same yesterday, today or tomorrow. Our bodies are continuing to renew themselves as cells wear out. Neither are we emotionally or experientially the same, but subject to change as we learn, discover and grow.

God on the other hand is not subject to change. Even though some writers and people believe they can change God's mind, they cannot. His will prevails in all things. Those who pray can pray for change in our world but God is already aware of our prayer even before we come to Him. He has made accommodation for that.

By virtue of God being eternal, He is outside of time and therefore is not subject to time. and for that reason, has no need to change. "So, the words greater, lessor, back, forward, up down cannot apply to God. God is the eternal God and remains unchanged and unchanging -that is, He is immutable." (A.W. Tozer, 1997)

What is known about God the Father is also attributable to the Son of God, Jesus. What is known about the Father and the Son is attributable to the Holy Spirit. It is critical to know and understand this because all of God is immutable. In Hebrews 13:8, we see this underwritten, "Jesus is the same yesterday and today and forever." Jesus the incarnate man did change being born as an infant and dying on a cross as an adult. However, He exists today both God and Incarnate man in a resurrected body, the promise to humanity of the resurrection of each of us.

➢ **Why is this important?** God is perfect and does not need to change anything either in His thought or in His action. Because He does not change, we can count on Him to answer prayers, keep His promises and to judge all perfectly. When God makes covenants with specific people they know He will not change His mind but will fulfill His covenants.

VI. God is Eternal:

➢ Duration through endless ages (Psalm 90:2; 93:2; 102:12; Ephesians 3:21)
➢ God is not bound by time. (Psalm 90:4; 2 Peter 3:8)

Psalm 90:2-4

> *"2 Before the mountains were born or you brought forth the whole world, from everlasting to everlasting you are God. 3 You turn people back to dust, saying, "Return to dust, you mortals." 4 A thousand years in your sight are like a day that has gone by, or like a watch in the night. (NIV)*

➢ Creator of the ages. (Hebrews 1:2; 11:3)

The fact that God is eternal means that He is unconcerned with time because He exists outside of time. Being outside of time then, means that He is capable to initiate time which He did. We see evidence that time exists by the changes of nights to days, days to weeks, and months to years.

We see this in the movement of the earth, the moon and the sun. However, there is one sense of time that has no physical relationship, but to which we all throughout the world accede. That measure of course is the week. We know the week as being seven days, but from where has that worldwide convention come? "In the Beginning God". Geneses 1 & 2 tell us that God gave us the week so that we might have rest from our work and that we would be dedicated to God in worship. We seemed to have forgotten the need for rest. The idea of being thankful to our creator who bestows upon us great benefits, seems to have slipped into insignificance as we market over 365 days a year. We do this to great harm to each of us. In the words of Bob Dylan, "Who are you going to serve?" Everyone has to choose. In how we spend our time in these things our service becomes evident.

➢ **Why is this important?** God is perfect in that He transcends all time and temporal limitations. He exists outside of time and in fact time was created by Him at creation. Because He exists outside of time, He has knowledge of all that will occur in time. Being eternal He knows the beginnings and endings of all things. With this knowledge he works events to His will while respecting our independent will. Furthermore, by this attribute, He can and does initiate life after death with rewards and punishment.

VII.   God is Omnipotent:

➢ God is perfect in that He can do all things consistent with the perfection of His being. God cannot or will not do anything that is contradictory to His being and nature.
➢ All things are possible with God. (Job 42:2; Psalm 115:3; Matthew 19:26; Mark 10:27; Luke 1:37; 18:27; Ephesians 1:11)

Luke 18:27

"27 Jesus replied, "What is impossible with man is possible with God."(NIV)

➢ All things God does are unlimited. (Psalm 90:4; 2 Peter 3:8)

➢ Creator of the ages. (Hebrews 1:2; 11:3)

God has to be all powerful, in order to be able to bring creation and the things that we know about and experience in our lives. All things, which exist must have been brought into being by someone or something greater than what exists. We know that this is God. He must be all powerful, exceeding what exists in power and effect or there would exist only nothing.

So, when we consider God, He must be all powerful, greater than every other thing. Being the first cause of everything means that nothing can be greater than He is. God's power is without limit and He is the source of all power that exists. He gives power but never is diminished by giving power, unlike batteries. God retains His fullness, whether He gives power to others or not. God sustains everything and perpetuates everything, without reduction in Himself. "So, let men turn their telescopes on the heaven and their microscopes on the molecules. Let them probe and search and tabulate and name and find and discover. I can dare say to them, 'I know the One who made all this. I'm personally acquainted with the One who made it.'" (A.W. Tozer, 1997)

➢ **Why is this important?** God is Powerful and able to do anything He wants. The only limits to God are those that are not within His nature. In terms of all other created things, God sustains them in their existence. All energy, all beings and all forms of matter emanate from God. His power is solely within Him and is not contingent on anything else. He alone is the originator of everything as He determines.

VIII.   God is Omniscient:

➢ God has perfect knowledge of everything, for all of time and beyond time. (Job 37:16; Daniel 2:22; Hebrews 4:13; Psalm 139:1-4)

Hebrews 4:13-14

"¹³ Nothing in all creation is hidden from God's sight. Everything is uncovered and laid bare before the eyes of him to whom we must give account. ¹⁴ Therefore, since we have a great high priest who has ascended into heaven, Jesus the Son of God, let us hold firmly to the faith we profess." (NIV)

➢ God Knows your motives and the heart of every decision. (1 Samuel 16:7; 1 Chronicles 28:9, 17; Jeremiah 17:10)
➢ God has a complete knowledge of events that have happened, are happening and will happen. (Isaiah 41:22-23; 42:9; 4:10; 44:7)

To say that God is omniscient, is to recognize that there is no limit to God's knowledge or understanding. You cannot hide from God in darkness or disguise. He knows every person, animal or insect that ever inhabited our planet. He is the one who designed them. He defines and resurrect you from your origin. God know everything there is to know. His recall is perfect and His understanding of "How" and "Why" are without any condition. He is perfect in his knowledge. Given this knowledge we must recognize that we can learn about God but we will never know Him fully because in His greatness He is ineffable. *(incapable of fully expressing in words)*

➢ **Why is this important?** The comprehensive and exhaustive condition of God's knowing makes Him the unique judge to be able to judge all things in a righteous and just way. No one will be able to say to God, "You don't know; you don't understand."

This also gives a clue as to what life after death is to be. It will be an eternity of discovery and learning about our God and His fullness. It will be an eternity of celebration and worship of the wonder that is God in His disclosure to each of us.

IX. God is Incorporeal:

➤ God has no body or is not made of matter. (incorporeal or having no body)
➤ God is Spirit (John 4:24)
➤ God is not man. (Numbers 23:19; 1 Samuel 15:29)

Numbers 23:19

¹⁹ God is not human, that he should lie, not a human being, that he should change his mind. Does he speak and then not act? Does he promise and not fulfill? *(NIV)*

God is incorporeal means that He has no physical body. This is because He is Spirit. A God with a physical body would be confined to space and time. A God as spirit is unconfined in all space and time so, He is capable to create freely. He can be present where and how he desires. The is no limits to a spiritual personal God.

➤ **Why is this important?** Implied by the doctrines of "self-existence, transcendence & omnipresence" is the power and intelligence to create something from His own capability and creative ability. His existence is significantly different from material beings and therefore His limitations are not related to this material world but only to His character. Furthermore, His existence is so intense that we humans cannot withstand His presence. He is also able to intervene into the material world at will.

X. God is One:

➤ God is perfectly a unique being. He exists as one infinite Being. There is only one God in (essence). He has revealed Himself in three persons: The Father, the Son and the Holy Spirit. All three are in perfect unity and are always present together but each manifests a personality of separateness while maintaining a unity of essence and knowledge. (Deuteronomy 6:4; Isaiah 43:10; 44:6, 8; 45:5-7, 21-22; Zechariah

14:9; 1 Corinthians 8:4-6; Galatians 3:20; Ephesians 4:5-6; 1 Timothy 2:5; James 2:19)

Deuteronomy 6:4-5

⁴ "Hear, O Israel: The LORD our God, the LORD is one. ⁵ You shall love the LORD your God with all your heart and with all your soul and with all your might. (ESV)

Isaiah 9:6

⁶ For to us a child is born, to us a son is given; and the government shall be upon his shoulder, and his name shall be called Wonderful Counselor, Mighty God, Everlasting Father, Prince of Peace. (ESV)

➢ All other gods are "so-called gods". (1 Corinthians 8:4-6; 1 Thessalonians 2:4)
➢ Satan, idols & the flesh of men are all false gods. (Psalm 96:4-5; 1 Corinthians 10:20; 2 Corinthians 4:4; Philippians 3:19)
➢ Wicked judges call themselves "god" in irony, not in their true nature. (Psalm 82:1, 6; John 10:34-36)

The oneness of God is important to the power and unity of the Father, Son and Holy Spirit. In all things, that God does He is unified. The Father is perfectly consistency with the Son and the Holy Spirit. They act in union with each other and are never unaware of each other. They love each other in this union and though they may perform differently it is always in union with each other and in full knowledge and agreement.

The Isaiah 9:6 reference is often recognized as a reference to Jesus Christ birth. However, the term, "Everlasting Father" can be translated as 'Father of everlasting ages. In that sense, we see the unity of God as portrayed as being involved in laying out the ages of creation even to this very day. Father, Son and Holy Spirit is the architect of history with clear understanding, God is in control of the playing out of history.

➤ **Why is this important?** The singularity of God in His being (essence) and the manifestations of His person make Him without equal in everything that exists. The manifestations of God the Father, God the Son and God the Holy Spirit make the knowing of God by humans more attainable through the communicable attributes. These attributes are demonstrated through and by the persons of the Tri-unity (Father, Son & Holy Spirit).

XI. God is Creator:

➤ God is the One and the only One who originated what we have as material existence today. By His unbounded power, His infinite existence and His unequalled knowledge; God has created infinite existence ex nililo (from nothing) and formed what the cosmos is now with all its component parts and governed by the laws that He has designed. (Genesis 1:1; Psalm 33:6; 102:25; Jeremiah 31:35; John 1:3; Romans 11:36; Hebrews 1:2; 11:3)

Jeremiah31:35

> *35 This is what the* LORD *says, he who appoints the sun to shine by day, who decrees the moon and stars to shine by night, who stirs up the sea so that its waves roar—the* LORD *Almighty is his name:* (NIV)

➤ God made all things by Himself. (Isaiah 44:24)

As creator, God is owner of all He has created. We see this reflected in the ownership of patents and copywrite in our world today. However, God's tile is over all in creation. His creation of humanity is of particular note because He made man in His own image. It is through this act that God gives man requirements and expectation in His relationship with humanity. He gave us the ability to think and reason. He gave us the ability to create from our ability to think. He gave us the ability to speak and thereby communicate with Him and with one another. God expects that we will enter into relationship with Him, as well as with one another.

➤ **Why is this important?** Because God is the originator of all that is created in the cosmos, He holds title to it. It is therefore His to do with as He pleases. It is by His authority that it is sustained throughout time.

Therefore, we need to recognize His title and authority and approach Him with a healthy respect and only upon the terms that He disclosed as His will.

XII.   God is Personal:

➤ God as the author of personhood in man and in the created cosmos, cannot be less than personal Himself
➤ Scripture everywhere assumes the personhood of God in the personal pronouns, in the records of Him speaking and acting willfully. (Genesis 1:3, 26; Hebrews 1:1-2)
➤ God gives Himself specific names and or titles. (Exodus 3:14; 15:26; 17:15; 31:13; Genesis 1:1; 2:4; 14:20; 15:2; 16:13; 17:1; 21:33; 22:14; Judges 6:24; 1 Samuel 1:3; Psalm 23:1; Jeremiah 23:1 & Ezekiel 48:25)

Exodus 3:14-15

> *[14] God said to Moses, "I AM WHO I AM. This is what you are to say to the Israelites: 'I AM has sent me to you.'" [15] God also said to Moses, "Say to the Israelites, 'The LORD, the God of your fathers—the God of Abraham, the God of Isaac and the God of Jacob—has sent me to you.' "This is my name forever, the name you shall call me from generation to generation.* (NIV)

The personhood of God underwrites our personhood. He made us like him, therefore we can have fellowship with one another. The love and unity of the God head is how we learn to enter into relationship with our family, friends, neighbours and business acquaintances. We can have significance in the lives of all these that we touch through relationship. Our personhood is like God's in that we strive for significance in relationship. Most animals do not have this, as they generally show no signs of deep personhood. They may have relationship through mutual support but in the beehive or the herd there is only togetherness in activity.

➤ **Why is this important?** God, being personal, can and does experience relationships with other persons and self-conscious beings like ourselves. Therefore, He will invite us into relationship with Himself both here and now and forever.

XIII.   God is Incomprehensible:

➤ God is incomprehensible. He is comprehensible in the sense of the concept of God but he cannot ever be fully or directly known as we are finite, and He is infinite.

➤ There is none like God. (Exodus 8:10; 9:14; 15:11; 2 Samuel 7:22; 1 Chronicles 17:20; 1 Kings 8:23; Isaiah 40:13-14,18, 25; 44:7; 56:5, 9; Jeremiah 10:6-7; Micah 7:18)

Isaiah 40:13-14

¹³ Who can fathom the Spirit of the LORD, *or instruct the* LORD *as his counselor? ¹⁴ Whom did the* LORD *consult to enlighten him, and who taught him the right way? Who was it that taught him knowledge, or showed him the path of understanding?* (NIV)

It is necessary to describe God, a Spirit, in analogical language in order for us to grasp some ideas about Him. (Ezekiel 1:26-28; Revelation 1:13-16) God can be known as the Son, Jesus reveals Him to us because the Son experienced manhood. (John 1:18; 11:25-27; Hebrews 1:1-3) However, the likelihood that we will ever attain full understanding of God, being infinite, while we are finite even after we enter eternity is limited.

➤ **Why is this important?** First the idea of incomprehensive needs some clarification. The idea of this term is that we can never come to a complete knowledge of God given that He is "infinite", and we are "finite". It is like trying to pour the Great Lakes into an 8-ounce glass.

The glass simply will never contain all that it is. This is important because it is one of the basic attributes of God. He, being infinite and by that incomprehensible to us, offers to enter a relationship with His people. Through this relationship we will be in an eternal learning and discovery of this God.

XIV.   God is Morally & otherwise Perfect:

➢ God is morally good and perfect in both His being and all His actions. (Genesis 1:31; Psalm 52:1; 100:5; 107:8; Nahum 1:7; Mark 10:18; Romans 8:28; 1 John 1:5)
➢ God's goodness is underived for it is an essential that He and only He possesses. He did not learn it from anyone nor did He have to acquire it through some test or learning. (Psalm 33:5; 118:1; 119:68; 139:14; 145:9, 15-16; Luke 2:14; Titus 2:11)

Psalm 33:4-5

⁴ For the word of the LORD *is right and true; he is faithful in all he does. ⁵ The* LORD *loves righteousness and justice; the earth is full of his unfailing love. (NIV)*

God is perfect because He lacks any imperfections. Nothing in His character, behavior or expectations is flawed in any way. God's excellence has no match nor is open to any criticism. No one can find fault with God because He has none. Those who criticize God either in His being, actions or words do so out of ignorance or willfulness. Those who set out to criticize God, often begin with one attribute such as Love and then try to build a strawman out of how the attribute is inconsistent with God's judgment and wrath. This approach is forgetting that all of God's attributed are in operation in all that God is and does. Clearly this strawman is missing a leg to stand upon.

God is incomparable because of His perfection. God is incomparable in His character, power and knowledge. With perfection we know there never be an error. Furthermore, this moral perfection underlines God's goodness. He is the very perfection of goodness. If you want to know what goodness is, then look to God's Son and how he lived here on earth among men.

➤ **Why is this important?** The Goodness of God permeates all that He is and all that He does. Therefore, there is a balance between His Holiness, His Righteousness, His Truth, His Love and His wraith. His judgments can be counted upon to advance from His goodness. (Exodus 33:19; Psalm 25:5-7; Micah 6:8) Furthermore, when we look at the fallen world with all its injustice and deceit, we know we can count on the goodness of God to direct us in this life. In His excellence God judges all. Those thinking that He will accept anything but perfection are mistaken. If we are unable to be perfect then we need a perfect Saviour. The Son of God came to save us by being perfect in human flesh in our place. He offers payment for our sins perfectly and offers a perfectly lived life that is available in place of our imperfect life.

➤ **Communicable attributes:**

Communicable attributes are qualities that we can understand and participate in or pursue in our lives. The difference in these between humans and God is in the order of magnitude and consistency. He is the definition of each of these and totally consistent. We are not.

I. Holiness:

➤ The Holiness of God is really describing the fact that God is set apart from all others. God is beyond anything we can imagine because He is different from us. (Exodus 3:5; 15:11; Leviticus 21:8; Joshua 24:19; 1 Chronicles 16:29; Psalm 22:3; 89:35; 96:9; Proverbs 9:10; Isaiah 6:3;)
➤ God's holiness is without blemish or shadow and emanates from His being into all judgments and action. (1 John 1:5; Exodus 15:11; Habakkuk 1:13)

Habakkuk 1:12-13

LORD, are you not from everlasting? My God, my Holy One, you will never die. You, LORD, have appointed them to execute judgment; you, my Rock, have ordained them to punish. ¹³ Your eyes are too pure to look on evil; you cannot tolerate wrongdoing. Why then do you tolerate the treacherous? Why are you silent while the wicked swallow up those more righteous than themselves? (NIV)

Holiness is being set apart from others in terms of purity. God is in a category all by Himself. There is no comparison on earth other than Jesus, who is the Son and filled with all excellence and purity as His Father. We cannot really comprehend the holiness of God given our fallen state. We are not good judges of holiness because most people never understand the vile nature and behaviour we are in reality. It is only God's great patience with fallen man that He does not destroy us in our daily thought life. What grade of truth do we expect from teachers, politicians, business leaders or children? No one really expect full disclosure from people nor do they give it in return.

This is not the way of God. His is truth and full disclosure on any issue with which He is concerned. God is morally excellent. He knows and judges from that excellence. God does not obfuscate nor shade the truth in anyway. God's standard is demonstrated by all that He is. His holiness does not change over time, neither increasing nor decreasing. He has disclosed to man that there is no change in him.

Micah 6:8

⁸ He has told you, O man, what is good; and what does the LORD require of you but to do justice, and to love kindness, and to walk humbly with your God? (ESV)

The picture often when talking about God's holiness is a fiery holiness. (Isaiah 6:2; Hebrews 12:39). There is no concession to God's holiness. He is entirely other from all of creation.

II. Righteousness:

➢ God is just or morally equal in the way of His judgments of all people & beings. (Isaiah 45:21; Zephaniah 3:5; Acts 17:31; Romans 3:36 and 1 Peter 1:17)

➢ God makes choices with fore knowledge that determine who are blessed and who are cursed. (Isaiah 42:1; 45:4; 65:22; Malachi 1:3; Matt.24:31; Rom. 9:13; 11:7; 11:28; 1 Peter 1:2, 10; 2:6; 2 John 13).

1 Peter 1:17-19

> *[17] Since you call on a Father who judges each person's work impartially, live out your time as foreigners here in reverent fear. [18] For you know that it was not with perishable things such as silver or gold that you were redeemed from the empty way of life handed down to you from your ancestors, [19] but with the precious blood of Christ, a lamb without blemish or defect. (NIV)*

God's righteousness must prevail in the context of all that He is. He will never pass over sin or downplay it. Actions or thoughts of man are judged by a standard that is never changing. They are frequently disclosed in scripture. Sin or iniquity is the unrighteous acts and the thoughts of humanity. Every sin must be paid for before a righteous judge, that God is. Man is unable to sacrifice enough to a swage our debt to God for our sin and for our iniquity. Therefore, man needs a Saviour who will pay for our sin and our iniquity. The only righteous Saviour is the Son of God who paid for sin and iniquity by dying on a cross for humanity. The gift of salvation is there as a free offer by acknowledging your need (Repentance) and asking the Saviour Jesus to accept you as a needy child of God.

➤ **Why is this important?** In view of the true and righteous judgments of God no one will be able to object to His decisions because they are equitable and factual. Furthermore, God judges from full knowledge of our acts and thought. He will never make an error so there never can be an appeal based upon the facts of each person's case. (Deuteronomy 32:4; Psalm 33:4)

III. Truth:

➤ God is true in all He is, says and does. He is consistent to His word and cannot, nor will He lie. (John 14:6; 17:17; Titus 1:2; and Hebrews 6:18)

> *(Titus 1:1-3) "Paul, a servant of God and an apostle of Jesus Christ to further the faith of God's elect and their knowledge of the truth that leads to godliness—² in the hope of eternal life, which God, who does not lie, promised before the beginning of time, ³ and which now at his appointed season he has brought to light through the preaching entrusted to me by the command of God our Savior,"(NIV)*

➤ God's truth is disclosed to us through our conscience and through the created order. It is also communicated through God's revelation in His word.

Truth is a precious commodity in our world. Unfortunately, it is so rare that being a commodity, it is more like a precious jewel. God speaks truth into the world. It has been captured by several people over the centuries and recorded. Because God is immutable His Truth never changes. Despite this, many people who cannot accept God's truth have rebelled by questioning or demeaning God's truth. Sadly, they do this to their own harm because the truth God has given us does not nor will it ever change.

We can count on God the Father, Christ the Son and the Holy Spirit to lead us by and into the truth, if we are open to their leading. Those that say to God that is your truth but my truth is xxx are bound to come to a fiery end. God's truth has never been changed over the full history of man.

➢ **Why is this important?** The truth of God will be demonstrated in all He says to humanity. Therefore, He will always ensure that His word is communicated correctly to all His people. (Mark 13:31; Luke 4:32; 2 Peter 1:12 and 2 Timothy 3:16-17) God's expectations are clear in His word, which does not change over time. It is also revealed in the conscience of man, which is evident and consistent across cultural boundaries. Furthermore, He will use only the true facts in all His judgments. (Psalm 103:6; John 5:30; Romans 2:2; Revelation 2:2)

IV. Loving:

➢ God is pure love that is sacrificial in nature and gives true benefit to others without any need for return. His love is not influenced by anything other than His being. (Deuteronomy 7:7-8; John 3:16 and Hebrews 12:6)

Deuteronomy 7:7-10

> *⁷ The* LORD *did not set his affection on you and choose you because you were more numerous than other peoples, for you were the fewest of all peoples. ⁸ But it was because the* LORD *loved you and kept the oath he swore to your ancestors that he brought you out with a mighty hand and redeemed you from the land of slavery, from the power of Pharaoh king of Egypt. ⁹ Know therefore that the* LORD *your God is God; he is the faithful God, keeping his covenant of love to a thousand generations of those who love him and keep his commandments. ¹⁰ But those who hate him he will repay to their face by destruction; he will not be slow to repay to their face those who hate him. ⁽ᴺᴵⱽ⁾*

➢ God's love is a deliberate choice that is not a response to any attributes of the object of love. (Romans 5:8)
➢ God's love is like Himself, everlasting. (Jeremiah 31:3 and Ephesians 1:4-5)

In the book of 1 John there is a treatise on the love of God. There is near universal acknowledgement that God is love. How that Love is demonstrated is found it 1 John. It is done by a comparison between God's love and human love in 1 Corinthians 13. According to John love comes from God and is self-sacrificial. Our is self-interest.

1 John 4:7-21 God is Love

> *⁷ Beloved, let us love one another, for love is from God, and whoever loves has been born of God and knows God. ⁸ Anyone who does not love does not know God, because God is love. ⁹ In this the love of God was made manifest among us, that God sent his only Son into the world, so that we might live through him. ¹⁰ In this is love, not that we have loved God but that he loved us and sent his Son to be the propitiation for our sins. ¹¹ Beloved, if God so loved us, we also ought to love one another. ¹² No one has ever seen God; if we love one another, God abides in us and his love is perfected in us. ¹³ By this we know that we abide in him and he in us, because he has given us of his Spirit. ¹⁴ And we have seen and testify that the Father has sent his Son to be the Savior of the world. ¹⁵ Whoever confesses that Jesus is the Son of God, God abides in him, and he in God. ¹⁶ So we have come to know and to believe the love that God has for us. God is love, and whoever abides in love abides in God, and God abides in him. ¹⁷ By this is love perfected with us, so that we may have confidence for the day of judgment, because as he is, so also are we in this world. ¹⁸ There is no fear in love, but perfect love casts out fear. For fear has to do with punishment, and whoever fears has not been perfected in love. ¹⁹ We love because he first loved us. ²⁰ If anyone says, "I love God," and hates his brother, he is a liar; for he who does not love his brother whom he has seen cannot love God whom he has not seen. ²¹ And this commandment we have from him: whoever loves God must also love his brother.*(ESV)*

Paul also gives us definition of Love that is often read and weddings. Love according to Paul is needed to make humans authentic. Love is self-sacrificial and is recognized by behaviors that are not love.

1 Corinthians 13:1-13 The Way of Love

13:1 If I speak in the tongues of men and of angels, but have not love, I am a noisy gong or a clanging cymbal. ² And if I have prophetic powers, and understand all mysteries and all knowledge, and if I have all faith, so as to remove mountains, but have not love, I am nothing. ³ If I give away all I have, and if I deliver up my body to be burned, but have not love, I gain nothing. ⁴ Love is patient and kind; love does not envy or boast; it is not arrogant ⁵ or rude. It does not insist on its own way; it is not irritable or resentful; ⁶ it does not rejoice at wrongdoing, but rejoices with the truth. ⁷ Love bears all things, believes all things, hopes all things, endures all things. ⁸ Love never ends. As for prophecies, they will pass away; as for tongues, they will cease; as for knowledge, it will pass away. ⁹ For we know in part and we prophesy in part, ¹⁰ but when the perfect comes, the partial will pass away. ¹¹ When I was a child, I spoke like a child, I thought like a child, I reasoned like a child. When I became a man, I gave up childish ways. ¹² For now we see in a mirror dimly, but then face to face. Now I know in part; then I shall know fully, even as I have been fully known. ¹³ So now faith, hope, and love abide, these three; but the greatest of these is love. (ESV)

We see by these two writers about God's love that it is a giving and a saving love. God's love is a selfless love. True love encourages and serves the loved one.

God's love is the sum of all love. God's love is eternal because God is eternal. God's love is righteous because God is righteous. God's Love is true because God is true. God's love is holy because God is holy. God's love is just because God is Just. Never forget that all that God is He displays in every way that He is; He never changes nor is diminishing.

➢ **Why is this important?** The love of God is a type of love that is seeking nothing back (Self sacrificial love – "Agape" in the Greek). Therefore, when God expresses love to beings or individuals He does so as a matter of grace without expectations. (1 John 16b-17) Furthermore, nothing can change the love expressed by God. Therefore nothing can separate us from His love (James 1:17; Romans 8:35-39). As an expression of God's love, He was willing to give His own Son to redeem humanity from their lost life in death. Death came as a result of sin and disobedience of man. Jesus Christ's own expression of the love is seen in that; He was willing to pay the price for those lost and dead in sin by His own volition.

> Love has its origin in who God is. All humanity owes our understanding of what love is to God. It is out of love that God created all we have on earth. It is out of this very same love that God foresaw the fall of Adam and Eve and began the process of redemptive history that winds its way through the Old Testament. It is out of God's love that He sends His only Son, Jesus of Nazareth, who is fully man and fully God, to redeem humanity by paying for their rebellion against God with His own blood, a sacrifice sufficient to meet the need of fallen humanity.

V. Merciful:

➢ God will show mercy to some and it is completely within His decision to show that mercy. He does so within His own decision and purpose often as an expression of His love. (Ephesians 2:4)

➢ God's mercy like God endures forever and will not change nor is subject to the actions of the recipients of that mercy. (Psalm 136:1; Psalm 59:16; Psalm 103:8-17)

➤ God shows general mercy upon the entire world by bringing rain in season and the changes of seasons and does this often without differentiation on the good and the evil. (Psalm 145:25; Acts 17:35 and Titus 3:5)

God is merciful and because He is infinite, His mercy is infinite. It cannot be lessened or diminished in anyway. God is the source of mercy. Mercy did not exist in our world until God created our world. The goodness of God is the desire in God to show and offer mercy. God takes no pleasure in the suffering of His people nor His enemies. (Ezekiel 33:11) At the same time, when he punishes, it is because he must meet His righteous judgement. The term "mercy" has a meaning of stooping down in kindness to an inferior, to have pity and compassion for them. Often we see God's mercy in connection with four activities:

✦ God hears their groaning in their suffering;
✦ God is moved with compassion;
✦ God remembers His covenant with those specific people;
✦ God is moved with compassion for His people and shows mercy.

It was the mercy of God the Father, which gave us the cross of Christ. His mercy opened the possibility of salvation and total forgiveness, by the cross of Christ. At the same time, a person can walk away from the mercy of God because he is a moral free agent. It takes repentence to stay under the wings of God's mercy. Those who reject God's merciful path to eternal life will never see it or benefit from it.

Exodus 33:19

And the Lord said, "I will cause all my goodness to pass in front of you, and I will proclaim my name, the Lord, in your presence. I will have mercy on whom I will have mercy, and I will have compassion on whom I will have compassion.(NIV)

➤ **Why is this important?** God chooses upon whom He will have mercy and whom He will show grace. Furthermore, it is because God is merciful that He sent His Son so that there would be a perfect way to salvation. (Exodus 33:19; Romans 9:15; 1 Timothy 5:21)

VI. Gracious:

➤ God is gracious to give unmerited favour to some even though they do not deserve it. (Acts 14:26; Romans 4:4 and 2 Thessalonians 1:12 Ephesians 2:8)

> *(Ephesians 2: 4-8)[4] But because of his great love for us, God, who is rich in mercy, [5] made us alive with Christ even when we were dead in transgressions—it is by grace you have been saved. [6] And God raised us up with Christ and seated us with him in the heavenly realms in Christ Jesus, [7] in order that in the coming ages he might show the incomparable riches of his grace, expressed in his kindness to us in Christ Jesus. [8] For it is by grace you have been saved, through faith—and this is not from yourselves, it is the gift of God—[9] not by works, so that no one can boast.[(NIV)]*

The term grace is defined as agreeable, pleasing, kindly, benevolent, courteous, condescending according to the Concise Oxford Dictionary. It is this idea of condescension of a greater One who stoops to favour some who are far below. Given that God is eternal and omnipotent, any benefit he provides humans is gracious. Anyone who thinks God owes them anything, does not understand the idea that the creator is the one with final authority over His creation. Those of His creation owe Him gratitude.

➤ **Why is this important?** Grace of God is not earned but is bestowed upon individuals. This means that your standing before God is from His goodness not your deeds nor your needs. (Romans 4:4, 16; 11:6)

VII.   Patience:

➤ God is immensely patient with His creation. When we see the goodness of God and compare it with the rebellion of man, we recognize that all are deserving retribution for their disobedience and ingratitude. (Acts 14:16-17; Acts 13:46; Genesis 6:3; Romans 1:19-26; 1 Peter 3:20)

➤ God's patience is tied to His mercy and goodness. In the scriptures this is described as being long suffering. (Exodus 34:6-7; Numbers 14:18; Psalm 86:15; 107:8; Nahum 1:3; Nehemiah 9:17; Romans 9:22)

Nehemiah 9:16-21

> *16 "But they and our fathers acted presumptuously and stiffened their neck and did not obey your commandments. 17 They refused to obey and were not mindful of the wonders that you performed among them, but they stiffened their neck and appointed a leader to return to their slavery in Egypt. But you are a God ready to forgive, gracious and merciful, slow to anger and abounding in steadfast love, and did not forsake them. 18 Even when they had made for themselves a golden calf and said, 'This is your God who brought you up out of Egypt,' and had committed great blasphemies, 19 you in your great mercies did not forsake them in the wilderness. The pillar of cloud to lead them in the way did not depart from them by day, nor the pillar of fire by night to light for them the way by which they should go. 20 You gave your good Spirit to instruct them and did not withhold your manna from their mouth and gave them water for their thirst. 21 Forty years you sustained them in the wilderness, and they lacked nothing. Their clothes did not wear out and their feet did not swell.* (ESV)

The patience of God is often described as long suffering. It is only because of the patience of God that He does not destroy us in our rebellion and disobedience. When man disobeys God's commandments, we incur the wrath of God. People do not really understand that His wrath is righteous wrath. He could sentence each of us to receive his wrath ending in our destruction but because of His mercy and patience He does not act against us now.

God continues to send rain and sun on the righteous and the unrighteous. He gives time to turn to Him for forgiveness and mercy. These are all demonstration of God's long suffering. Furthermore, He knows who will accept His offer and who will reject it. In giving the rejectors time, His demonstrated His patience and mercy. There will come a day when all accounts will be called to appear before the Righteous Judge. What will be given, in each of our cases, is the truth of how long-suffering God has been in enduring our lives before Him.

➤ **Why is this important?** The long suffering of God holds back His just wrath. Without God's patience we would be all wiped from the face of the earth at our first rebellious act against God's law. (Genesis 9:12-13; Lamentations 3:22; Psalm 103:8-17; Romans 1:28-2:4; 2 Peter 3:9)

VIII. Wrath:

➤ God's moral perfection requires Him to show displeasure against anything that is contrary to His moral purpose. (Deuteronomy 32:39-41; Psalm 2:1-12; 76:4-10; Isaiah 13:9-13; Mark 10:18; Romans 2:5; 1 John 1:5)

Psalm 76: 4-10

You are radiant with light, more majestic than mountains rich with game. ⁵ The valiant lie plundered, they sleep their last sleep; not one of the warriors can lift his hands. ⁶ At your rebuke, God of Jacob, both horse and chariot lie still. ⁷ It is you alone who are to be feared. Who can stand before you when you are angry? ⁸ From heaven you pronounced judgment, and the land feared and was quiet—⁹ when you, God, rose up to judge, to save all the afflicted of the land. ¹⁰ Surely your wrath against mankind brings you praise, and the survivors of your wrath are restrained. (NIV)

➤ God is not indifferent to sin. He is specific in defining those things he desires and those things which offend His goodness. He created all things "good" and some things "very good". So, when unrighteousness, which is an act or thought that offends His goodness occurs, He is required to judge that act or thought. Both His laws which set the boundaries of moral goodness and His judgements can be counted upon to reflect the best possible outcomes. His judgments are perfect. (Genesis 3:14-19, 23; Psalm 19:1-14; Romans 9:22-24; 2:14; Titus 2:11)

Humanity does not well understand the wrath of God. They see glimpses of it in disasters like tsunami, earthquakes and great bouts of pestilence. However, there are several examples given us in scripture that should bring us to the recognition that God's wrath is true and has everlasting consequences. The first is the worldwide flood as described in Genesis chapters 5-9. God destroyed all humanity except 8 people as named in chapter 8.

The second demonstration is in the book of Exodus where God call Moses to go to Pharaoh, to demand that he release God's people from slavery. God punishes Egypt with ten plagues to change Pharoah's mind. Pharoah refuse until the tenth plague, wherein God takes the first-born son from every family and kill them in one night. Pharoah relents and sends them away. Afterward he has a change of mind and pursues the Israelites out into the desert, surrounding them with their backs against the Red Sea. God opens a passageway through the sea but when pharaoh and his army enter into it, God wraith is again demonstrated by closing the sea over them all drowning the entire army.

God demonstrated His wrath against individuals, kings and people groups throughout scripture. We must understand that God's wrath will be directed at those who oppose Him. What is not certain is when.

God has specifically sentenced Satan and his minions to a captivity in hell. This destination is certain but where and when are currently unknown. Those who think that Hell is anything you might want not to fear, it is the height of foolishness. God has set it aside for anyone who does not want to spend their eternity in the company of God. Hell is a place where those who refused God's invitation to salvation or were unrepentant in their rebellion against God. It was originally designed to be the place of imprisonment of Satan. The gates of Hell are locked from the inside by people & beings who have refused God's grace. Judging from the long history of God's wrath, it is not a place you would want to spend any time there, let alone eternity.

➤ **Why is this important?** The sovereignty of God is confronted by rebellion when sin occurs. Therefore, there is a balance between His Holiness, His Righteousness, His Truth, His Love and His Wrath. His judgments can be counted upon to advance from His goodness and establish His sovereignty for all time. He isolates the beings who are designed by His righteous judgments for His wrath. (Ezekiel 33:11; 2 Peter 2:4-11; Hebrews 10:30-31) *(NIV)*

The Great Misunderstanding:

There are many misunderstandings of God because people look to one or two attributes of God and think, well if God is merciful and loving, then hell cannot be true. The misunderstanding is that while God is merciful and loving he is also Holy, Righteous and Just. In that context, **each and every** one of the attributes come into play when God makes provisions for humanity.

Genesis 1:28-31

Mankind's beginning in the protected Garden: ²⁸ *God blessed them and said to them, "Be fruitful and increase in number; fill the earth and subdue it. Rule over the fish in the sea and the birds in the sky and over every living creature that moves on the ground."* ²⁹ *Then God said, "I give you every seed-bearing plant on the face of the whole earth and every tree that has fruit with seed in it. They will be yours for food.* ³⁰ *And to all the beasts of the earth and all the birds in the sky and all the creatures that move along the ground— everything that has the breath of life in it—I give every green plant for food." And it was so.* ³¹ *God saw all that he had made, and it was very good.* (NIV)

He began Man as a family unit of Adam and Eve, with only one condition to their good life, in the garden. The original concept was that perfect human life was to be eternal. It was conditional upon their relationship with God, where it is described that God walked with them in the cool of the evening:

Genesis 1:15-17

¹⁵ *The* LORD *God took the man and put him in the Garden of Eden to work it and take care of it.* ¹⁶ *And the* LORD *God commanded the man, "You are free to eat from any tree in the garden;* ¹⁷ *but you must not eat from the tree of the knowledge of good and evil, for when you eat from it you will certainly die."*(NIV)

God called them to obedience to **the one and only command** "You must not eat of the tree of Good and evil for when you do you will surely die." This may seem to be a strong punishment for stealing fruit, but what is missed is that not only was this a condition of blessing and provision of God, but Adam and Eve are the progenitors of what will be the whole human race. If they disobey God, they will bring down upon their offspring, which is each of us, the curse of death. This is exactly what happened. It is why, we all die. It is also why; we struggle with understanding who God is.

However, in **_Chapter 3_** of Genesis, we see a God provision for our salvation in the pronouncement of God to the pair and to the tempter.

¹⁴ *So the* LORD *God said to the serpent, "Because you have done this, "Cursed are you above all livestock and all wild animals! You will crawl on your belly and you will eat dust all the days of your life.* ¹⁵ *And I will put enmity between you*

and the woman, and between your offspring and hers; he will crush your head, and you will strike his heel."(NIV)

Sin is defined in scripture in three ways. First, it is defined as a "Debt to be paid". Second, it is defined as "Enmity with God". In other words, we are at war with God in what we have said, done or thought. Third, it is described as a "Crime against God". For anyone to think they can cover their debt, enmity or crime with good works, do not understand the complex, just and holy nature of God.

In this, God is setting in place a future, whereby He will send a Saviour to reverse the effects of the curse of death and slavery to sin. For a Holy and just God, ALL sin or disobedience to His laws must be paid for in kind. The original disobedience brought death and the salvation will also bring death to pay for it. That death is God's own Son, Jesus of Nazareth, who will redeem all humanity from their fallen state. Let there be no misunderstanding among the people of the earth. God demands payment for the debt we owe. He asked our ancestors, to obey just one Commandment. Adam failed and caused an inheritance of sin. We, in our turn, rebelled and have committed our own sins. It may have been against one Command or Ten Commandments, but where we once were people who loved and fellowshipped with God face to face; we are all guilty of rebellion against a Holy God.

PART 4

Who is Jesus of Nazareth?

This question has stirred up controversy for almost two thousand years. Some say he was a great teacher. Muslims credit Jesus as a great prophet. Some say he was a mad man who had a god complex. Some say that he was the Son of God. So, in order to answer this question, we should look at what those who knew him. What do they say about him? What did they record as the sayings of Jesus? First let us look at some of the critics of Jesus who do not accept him to be either a great teacher or a historical holy man sent to earth by God.

A. <u>The Jesus Seminar</u>

There has emerged a group who call themselves the Jesus Seminar, who have about 150 members. They say that they have been in search of the "historic Jesus". They voted on what in scripture reflects the true historical Jesus, based on their personal view of scriptures and miracles.

> *The Seminar is comprised of liberal Catholics and Protestants, Jews, and atheists. Most are male professors, though their number includes a pastor, a filmmaker, and three women.*

About half are graduates of Harvard, Claremont, or Vanderbilt divinity schools.[2]

They did this between 1985 and 2005, which was the year of the death of the founder Robert Funk. Their research was based upon reading the deeds and sayings recorded in the four books of the New Testament - Matthew, Mark, Luke & John. Their method was to vote with beads whether they believed that Jesus said this or that. They also voted on whether Jesus did the things recorded. They got a lot of publicity in doing this over the 20 years of the group. However, if you rule out all miracles and any reference to God as they have done, one will have to consider their approach to be biased. Furthermore, to judge the record from afar without giving weight to the witness records, which were all within forty years of the events, it is presumptuous if not foolhardy.

B. <u>Jesus is just a great teacher:</u>

There is little doubt about the historical fact that Jesus of Nazareth lived and died at the time of Pilate, Caesar Augustus (at his birth) and Tiberius. Pilate was the governor of Judah, during Jesus three-year mission and death. There are also historical records that Jesus recruited twelve men to be in his close group of disciples, who lived with Him and knew Him intimately. These are the sources of much of the historical record about the actions and saying of Jesus. There is also sizeable historical agreement that one of these, Judas, betrayed Jesus for thirty pieces of silver and afterward commits suicide.

So, when we look at the teachings of Jesus, we will need to look to the truth record to see what Jesus did and said to judge whether he was only a "good teacher", was self-deluded, was a fraud, or is the Son of God. If Jesus says and does things that point to his being the Son of God, then He is what He says He is. However, if he says and does these things, but is not or cannot be the Son of God, then he must be deluded. He cannot be a "good teacher because he would be guilty of conscious lying". So, based

---

[2] Geisler, N. L. (1999). <u>Jesus Seminar</u>. In *Baker encyclopedia of Christian apologetics* (p. 386). Grand Rapids, MI: Baker Books.

on this reasoning He cannot be just considered to be a "good teacher" because in His own words:

Mark 10:16-18

> *17 As Jesus started on his way, a man ran up to him and fell on his knees before him. "Good teacher," he asked, "what must I do to inherit eternal life?" 18 "Why do you call me good?" Jesus answered. "No one is good—except God alone." (NIV)*

Only God is Good. So, in Jesus' opinion, there is a difference between man and God. This does not sound like a man who is deluded. Furthermore, it is making a distinction between his teaching and the goodness of God. Therefore, we concluded that Jesus is not admitting to being a "good teacher" nor is he illustrating he is under delusions of grandeur.

C. Did Jesus ever say He was God?

The short answer to this is yes! However, often you need to interpret his declaration by how the first century audience reacts. For example, in *John 5:17-18* we read,

> *17 But Jesus answered them, "My Father is working until now, and I am working." 18 This was why the Jews were seeking all the more to kill him, because not only was he breaking the Sabbath, but he was even calling God his own Father, making himself equal with God. (ESV)*

The Jewish authorities when questioning Jesus as to why He thought that it is acceptable to heal on the Sabbath, hear Jesus' response, then they conclude that Jesus is saying God is His Father. They set out to kill Him for the crime of blasphemy.

In Luke 5, Jesus is seated in a house which is packed with people listening to Him teach. Some men have brought a paralytic man who is confined to bed. They break open the roof and lower him down to Jesus in the crowd.

¹⁹ but finding no way to bring him in, because of the crowd, they went up on the roof and let him down with his bed through the tiles into the midst before Jesus. ²⁰ And when he saw their faith, he said, "Man, your sins are forgiven you." ²¹ And the scribes and the Pharisees began to question, saying, "Who is this who speaks blasphemies? Who can forgive sins but God alone?" ²² When Jesus perceived their thoughts, he answered them, "Why do you question in your hearts? ²³ Which is easier, to say, 'Your sins are forgiven you,' or to say, 'Rise and walk'? ²⁴ But that you may know that the Son of Man has authority on earth to forgive sins"—he said to the man who was paralyzed—"I say to you, rise, pick up your bed and go home." ²⁵ And immediately he rose up before them and picked up what he had been lying on and went home, glorifying God. ²⁶ And amazement seized them all, and they glorified God and were filled with awe, saying, "We have seen extraordinary things today." (ESV)

Here Jesus heals the man but then forgives his sin also. The Jews knew and comment on this as blasphemy too. But Jesus silences them with the question which is easier "to forgive sins" or "to heal"? He miraculously commands the man to get up and walk which he does. By virtue of implication of which is easier, Jesus proves to the audience that he is in fact the Son of God.

Next Jesus is teaching, as part of the sermon on the mount, as recorded in *Matthew 7*.

²¹ "Not everyone who says to me, 'Lord, Lord,' will enter the kingdom of heaven, but only the one who does the will of my Father who is in heaven. ²² Many will say to me on that day, 'Lord, Lord, did we not prophesy in your name and in your name drive out demons and in your name perform many miracles?'²³ Then I will tell them plainly, 'I never knew you. Away from me, you evildoers!' (NIV)

As we see here, Jesus is claiming to have judgment authority over who will enter the kingdom of Heaven. Who but God can claim authority in heaven?

Next, we see that trial of Jesus before the Sanhedrin, the high court of the Jewish nation. Before they take him to the Roman authorities (Herod & Pilate) for trial in the only court which had the authority to sentence death. From *Luke 22,*

> *⁶⁶ At daybreak the council of the elders of the people, both the chief priests and the teachers of the law, met together, and Jesus was led before them. ⁶⁷ "If you are the Messiah," they said, "tell us."*

> *Jesus answered, "If I tell you, you will not believe me, ⁶⁸ and if I asked you, you would not answer. ⁶⁹ But from now on, the Son of Man will be seated at the right hand of the mighty God."*

> *⁷⁰ They all asked, "Are you then the Son of God?" He replied, "You say that I am."*

> *⁷¹ Then they said, "Why do we need any more testimony? We have heard it from his own lips."* (NIV)

The Sanhedrin find Jesus guilty of claiming to be the Son of God. A guilty verdict for telling the truth because the Jews believed no one could be the Son of God. In John 10, Jesus is responding to the question put to him by the temple authorities as to whether He is the Messiah or not.

John 10:22-33 Further Conflict Over Jesus' Claims

²² Then came the Festival of Dedication at Jerusalem. It was winter, ²³ and Jesus was in the temple courts walking in

Solomon's Colonnade. ²⁴ The Jews who were there gathered around him, saying, "How long will you keep us in suspense? If you are the Messiah, tell us plainly."

²⁵ Jesus answered, "I did tell you, but you do not believe. The works I do in my Father's name testify about me, ²⁶ but you do not believe because you are not my sheep. ²⁷ My sheep listen to my voice; I know them, and they follow me. ²⁸ I give them eternal life, and they shall never perish; no one will snatch them out of my hand. ²⁹ My Father, who has given them to me, is greater than all; no one can snatch them out of my Father's hand. ³⁰ I and the Father are one."

³¹ Again his Jewish opponents picked up stones to stone him, ³² but Jesus said to them, "I have shown you many good works from the Father. For which of these do you stone me?"

³³ "We are not stoning you for any good work," they replied, "but for blasphemy, because you, a mere man, claim to be God."(NIV)

Jesus confesses that He has told them that He is the messiah in His teaching and in the extraordinary works of healings. Yet they refuse to accept that He is the messiah. He then says that this does not surprise Him, because only the sheep of His fold recognize Him. They are given to Him by His father and He and the Father are one. The authorities then pick-up stones to stone Him to death again "because you, a mere man claim to be God."

D. __Does Jesus act like God:__

The Israelites revered the scriptures, especially the Pentateuch (the first five books of the Bible). They recognized that it came from Moses while he was on Mount Sinai, communing with God. Therefore no one in their mind could be allowed to change the law but God Himself. They reason God was the One who gave it to Moses and Israel in the first place.

However, along comes this Jesus and He teaches "you have heard it said" or "it is written but I say to you…" This is described in Matthew 7 best:

> [28] *When Jesus had finished saying these things, the crowds were amazed at his teaching,* [29] *because he taught as one who had authority, and not as their teachers of the law.* (NIV)

There were plenty of teachers of the law who taught by referencing other teachers before them, in explaining the law and the prophets. Jesus on the other hand does not reference other teachers at all. He is the only teacher of the law who is an authority on to His own. By doing this, Jesus is saying that He and the Father are of one accord in His interpretation. Only God would dare do this.

Second, Jesus does miracles of healings and raising people from the dead. Who can roll back death but God? In particular, Jesus raises Lazarus after he has been in the tomb for 4 days. Lazarus comes out covered in the wrapping of the grave and continues to live several decades longer only, to die again on the island of Cyprus. In the town of Lamaca, a sarcophagus was found in 890 AD, that bears the inscription "Lazarus – four days dead, friend of Jesus". Beside Lazarus, Jesus is recorded as raising the following from the dead:

✦ Jairus' Daughter: Luke 8:49–56;
✦ Widow of Nain's Son: Luke 7:11–17;
✦ Jesus himself: Matthew 28:1-20; Mark 16:1-20; Luke 24:1-49; John 20:1-21:25.

The widow's son was likely dead at least two day and the daughter of Jairus was dead only hours. Jesus himself was likely in the grave over about 38-40 hours after having suffered several beatings & floggings. Finally, He endured several hours of excruciating punishment on a cross before dying.

Third, Matthew recounts a boat trip on the Sea of Galilee. Jesus is asleep in the stern of the boat and the disciples are rowing it across the lake when a storm breaks upon them. The boat is being tossed around and the waves are breaking over the sides of the boat. The disciples wake Jesus in fear for their lives, as they are in danger of sinking. Jesus changes everything for the disciples who are then confronted with this unfathomable recognition,

Matthew 8:25-27

25 The disciples went and woke him, saying, "Lord, save us! We're going to drown!"

26 He replied, "You of little faith, why are you so afraid?" Then he got up and rebuked the winds and the waves, and it was completely calm.

27 The men were amazed and asked, "What kind of man is this? Even the winds and the waves obey him!"(NIV)

"What kind of man" is the right assessment, because no ordinary man can speak to a storm and cause it to cease – only the Son of God.

Fourth, as we have already pointed out, the Jews were ultra conservative when it came to recognizing and keeping the Sabbath. The Sabbath being given in the Genesis 1 & 2 accounts of creation. The teachers of the law saw the Sabbath as being holy to the Lord God, as a sacrifice unto Him. They did not see the Sabbath as a day of rest given to man to commune with his God. In Luke 6,

6:1 One Sabbath Jesus was going through the grain fields, and his disciples began to pick some heads of grain, rub them in their hands and eat the kernels. 2 Some of the Pharisees asked, "Why are you doing what is unlawful on the Sabbath?"

3 Jesus answered them, "Have you never read what David did when he and his companions were hungry? 4 He entered the house of God, and taking the consecrated bread, he ate what is lawful only for priests to eat. And he also gave some to his companions." 5 Then Jesus said to them, "The Son of Man is Lord of the Sabbath."(NIV)

Jesus teaches that their error has caused them to become focused on the wrong things in the Sabbath. They are scandalized when Jesus declares himself as the Lord of the Sabbath. Further to this quote above, Jesus in all the four gospel accounts often uses this term "the Son of Man." Many see this to be a claim of being only human. However, this is in fact a reference to Daniel 7:13-14, which all the educated Jews would immediately recognize.

> *¹³ "In my vision at night I looked, and there before me was one like a son of man, coming with the clouds of heaven. He approached the Ancient of Days and was led into his presence. ¹⁴ He was given authority, glory and sovereign power; all nations and peoples of every language worshiped him. His dominion is an everlasting dominion that will not pass away, and his kingdom is one that will never be destroyed.* (NIV)*

As we see in this vision, Daniel had 700 years before the coming of Christ Jesus, the "Son of man" was "one" who is coming with the clouds of heaven. He approaches the "Ancient of Days" (Who is God) who gives Him authority, glory and sovereign power. Furthermore, "all nations & peoples of every language worshipped Him. His kingdom will not pass away and will never be destroyed. Who but the Son of God fits that description? His coming is seen by Daniel in advance of His birth, some 700 years later in a small town called Bethlehem outside of Jerusalem. His ascension to the throne is seen which comes after His death and resurrection. Fifty (50) days after Jesus miraculous resurrection, He returns to heaven. This is seen by Stephen, the first martyred Christians in Acts 7. Stephen testifies to the Jewish court, as their continuous disobedience to the law and to God the Father in that they have now killed the Son of God. Stephen too has a vision as he is being stoned:

Acts 7:54-56 The Stoning of Stephen

> *⁵⁴ Now when they heard these things they were enraged, and they ground their teeth at him. ⁵⁵ But he, full of the Holy*

Spirit, gazed into heaven and saw the glory of God, and Jesus
standing at the right hand of God. ⁵⁶ And he said, "Behold, I
see the heavens opened, and the Son of Man standing at the
right hand of God." (ESV)

The kingdom of God is complete now in Heaven, with Jesus sitting at the right hand of God, having been given complete authority over the earth. Going forward in time the Kingdom of God(heaven) is being established on earth forever. It will be finally complete, when Jesus comes again for the second time, to judge all humanity for all time.

Conclusion:

When we examine what Jesus said and how the Jewish establishment react, we can conclude that yes, Jesus did say emphatically and by implication that He was divine in nature, the Son of God. There are also **several actions** recorded of Jesus that also support that this was no ordinary man. So, the conclusion I came to early on that only someone who was both man and God could possibly have done these things.

A. What do the Old Testament Prophets say about Jesus?

Most of the prophets from the old Testament have descriptions of the coming of the Messiah. There are 39 books in the Old Testament and 27 in the New Testament.

➢ **Isaiah:**

In ***Isaiah 9:6-7***, says the following about who He is and why He is coming:

> *"For to us a child is born, to us a son is given, and the*
> *government will be on his shoulders. And he will be called*
> *Wonderful Counselor, Mighty God, Everlasting Father,*
> *Prince of Peace. Of the increase of his government and peace*
> *there will be no end. He will reign on David's throne and*
> *over his kingdom, establishing and upholding it with justice*

and righteousness from that time on and forever. The zeal of the Lord Almighty will accomplish this." (NIV)

First, by this prophecy we see this child is given the government of an entity, that can only be greater than a nation state because it is endowed by God Himself. Furthermore, this child is endowed as "wonderful counselor, mighty God, everlasting Father & Prince of Peace ". What Isaiah is saying by implication is that God is sending one who is "of Himself, a Son, given to rule that world". You think this odd because there are two thousand years roughly, between the birth of Jesus and now. Even though there is no visible evidence that there is such an authority ruling over the world, you would be looking in the wrong place with myopic vision. God does rule over everything as we have seen in question TWO. We will see that Jesus does admit that He has been given all authority from His Father-God. Some humans continue in the belief that this life is all that there is. If there is such a thing as eternal life, then the 60 to 90 years versus infinity is nothing! God and Jesus His Son take the eternal view of history.

➢ **Micah:**

In *Micah 5:2-5*, we see that again the prophets call for a specific place where this Messiah would be born.

> *² But you, O Bethlehem Ephrathah, who are too little to be among the clans of Judah, from you shall come forth for me one who is to be ruler in Israel, whose coming forth is from of old, from ancient days. ³ Therefore he shall give them up until the time when she who is in labor has given birth; then the rest of his brothers shall return to the people of Israel. ⁴ And he shall stand and shepherd his flock in the strength of the* LORD, *in the majesty of the name of the* LORD *his God. And they shall dwell secure, for now he shall be great to the ends of the earth. And he shall be their peace. (ESV)*

While the Jewish authorities dismissed Jesus because they thought he came from Nazareth, we know in both Matthew and Luke that Jesus was born in Bethlehem because of a proclamation by a Caesar Augustus, to hold a Roman Census.

➢ Jeremiah:

In *Jeremiah 23:5-6*, the prophets call for this Messiah to be born of the line of David.

> *"⁵ The day is coming, declares the Lord, when I will raise up to David a righteous branch, a King who will reign wisely and do what is just and right in the land. ⁶ In his days Judah will live in safety. This is the name by which he is called: The Lord Our Righteousness.* "(NIV)

How is it possible that this child would be our righteousness? This is in fact what Jesus says, he came to earth to provide for humanity – RIGHTEOUNESS!!! As we will see this righteousness is not our own but is bought with a price through His death on a Roman cross. Furthermore, in both the genealogies of Jesus, given by Luke & Matthew it is clear that Jesus is in the royal line of David.

➢ Moses:

After Moses has led the children of Israel out into the wilderness and at Mount Sinai, they encounter the presence of God and are frightened by what they encountered. They continue to show fear, but do not trust in His provision. They then spend forty years in the wilderness until they are finally ready to enter the promised land. They ask Moses to send them a prophet like Moses, who is born from their tribe, can speak with God and will lead them in a human way, with the power of God, which will not be so frightening. Moses speaks of one who will come that will suit these requirements.

Deuteronomy 18:15-19

¹⁵ The Lord your God will raise up for you a prophet like me from among your own brothers. You must listen to him. ¹⁶ For this is what you asked of the Lord your God at Horeb on the day of the assembly when you said, "Let us not hear the voice of the Lord our God nor see this great fire anymore, or we will die." ¹⁷ The Lord said to me: "What they say is good. ¹⁸ I will raise up for them a prophet like you from among their brothers; I will put my words in his mouth, and he will tell them everything I command him. ¹⁹ If anyone does not listen to my words that the prophet speaks in my name, I myself will call him to account. (NIV)

While God will send many prophets and judges to the children of Israel, none of them will be like Jesus of Nazareth. Jesus speaks as if he has authority. When the people say this about Jesus, they are saying no teacher has ever had the authority to make law and interpret the scriptures, in a way that their understanding will be greater. They are admitting that Jesus has the authority greater, than Moses, who brought them the Law.

Conclusion:

There are many more of the old testament writers who speak about this Jesus, to attest to what He would be like and what He would do. These are three examples of witnesses who speak from before His coming to earth. They give the scripture readers warning to be ready for His coming. Let us look at those who walked with Him and learned from Him. In the three years when Jesus taught in Judea & Samaria & the surrounding areas of Palestine (Israel).

A. New Testament

What do the New Testament writers say about Jesus? After all they are writing as eyewitnesses of what Jesus said and did. They are writing within twenty to thirty years of Jesus death and resurrection. Furthermore, all the new Testament writers will die a martyr's death with the exception of John the apostle who will be imprisoned and die of old age.

➢ Matthew:

This child will not be an ordinary child but has a destiny of ruling the world and bring peace. This is reinforced by Matthew, the tax collector, in the New Testament. In Matthew's commentary on the above passage from Isaiah, in Matthew 1:22-23 we see that the birth of Jesus:

> *"²²All this took place to fulfill what the Lord had said through the prophet. ²³ The virgin will be with child and will give birth to a son and they will call him Immanuel which means "God with us."(NIV)*

Matthew says not only does the writing of Isaiah apply to Jesus, but the boy who was called Jesus by Mary & Joseph is to be called Immanuel. "Immanuel" means God with us. The idea that this, Messiah brings peace is seen in the context of world history and it seems that the world has been at war ever since Cain & Abel. Shortly after the first pair, Adam & Eve, are sent out of the garden, the early offspring "Cain & Able" are waring to the point that Cain murders his brother recording the first murder on earth. So, it has been ever since.

However, there is peace on earth for those who know Him, Jesus. This is peace with God in that we are no longer under His damnation for our disobedience to His laws in our lives. We are no longer in debt to God for our sin. We are no longer in enmity with God and our crimes against Him are paid in full. Anyone who considers the ten Commandments and the Love your neighbour as yourself, cannot realistically say they fully obey God for that obedience is accounted in thought life and deeds all together.

➢ Luke:

Luke and Matthew are the only two writers who speak about the extraordinary birth of Jesus. However, I want to take you to a specific example of Jesus teaching and performing remarkable feats. This is captured in Luke 9.

Luke 9:10-17 Jesus Feeds the Five Thousand

[10] When the apostles returned, they reported to Jesus what they had done. Then he took them with him and they withdrew by themselves to a town called Bethsaida, [11] but the crowds learned about it and followed him. He welcomed them and spoke to them about the kingdom of God, and healed those who needed healing. [12] Late in the afternoon the Twelve came to him and said, "Send the crowd away so they can go to the surrounding villages and countryside and find food and lodging, because we are in a remote place here." [13] He replied, "You give them something to eat." They answered, "We have only five loaves of bread and two fish—unless we go and buy food for all this crowd." [14] (About five thousand men were there.) But he said to his disciples, "Have them sit down in groups of about fifty each." [15] The disciples did so, and everyone sat down. [16] Taking the five loaves and the two fish and looking up to heaven, he gave thanks and broke them. Then he gave them to the disciples to distribute to the people. [17] They all ate and were satisfied, and the disciples picked up twelve basketfuls of broken pieces that were left over. (NIV)

This illustrated several remarkable things. The first, is that Jesus is able to multiply a few fish and loafs into a banquet for thousands. When all are fed, he asks the disciples to gather up the remainder. They have twelve baskets full. That is a reminder to each of the twelve that Jesus is capable of providing for their needs in ways they cannot comprehend.

This is also a reproduction of the way that God feeds the children of Israel in their forty years in the desert land. That miracle happened during Moses' time with the provision of manna in the wilderness.

> ➤ **Mark:**

Let us look at the famous record of Jesus cleansing of the temple ground. Here is Mark's account of Jesus teaching and actions.

Mark 11:15-18

15 On reaching Jerusalem, Jesus entered the temple courts and began driving out those who were buying and selling there. He overturned the tables of the money changers and the benches of those selling doves, 16 and would not allow anyone to carry merchandise through the temple courts. 17 And as he taught them, he said, "Is it not written: 'My house will be called a house of prayer for all nations'? But you have made it 'a den of robbers.'" 18 The chief priests and the teachers of the law heard this and began looking for a way to kill him, for they feared him, because the whole crowd was amazed at his teaching. (NIV)

This is radical teaching. Jesus is claiming ownership of the Temple in Jerusalem. The specific area he is cleansing is the courtyard of the Gentiles. The teachers of the law and the priests had turned it into a marketplace for anyone wanting to come and make a sacrifice or pay a tithe.

➢ **John:**

All through the book of John are bold references to the divinity of Jesus. In John 8, Jesus is engulfed in a discussion with several Jewish authorities. They are claiming that Jesus is a fraud and making claims of authority that they will not recognize. They question His birth and His motivation. Jesus' answer is a claim that astounds the authorities. "before Abraham was, I Am".

John 8:48- 59 Jesus' Claims About Himself

48 The Jews answered him, "Aren't we right in saying that you are a Samaritan and demon-possessed?"

49 "I am not possessed by a demon," said Jesus, "but I honor my Father and you dishonor me. 50 I am not seeking glory for myself; but there is one who seeks it, and he is the judge. 51

Very truly I tell you, whoever obeys my word will never see death."

⁵²At this they exclaimed, "Now we know that you are demon-possessed! Abraham died and so did the prophets, yet you say that whoever obeys your word will never taste death. ⁵³Are you greater than our father Abraham? He died, and so did the prophets. Who do you think you are?"

⁵⁴Jesus replied, "If I glorify myself, my glory means nothing. My Father, whom you claim as your God, is the one who glorifies me. ⁵⁵Though you do not know him, I know him. If I said I did not, I would be a liar like you, but I do know him and obey his word. ⁵⁶Your father Abraham rejoiced at the thought of seeing my day; he saw it and was glad."

⁵⁷"You are not yet fifty years old," they said to him, "and you have seen Abraham!"

⁵⁸"Very truly I tell you," Jesus answered, "before Abraham was born, I am!" ⁵⁹At this, they picked up stones to stone him, but Jesus hid himself, slipping away from the temple grounds. (NIV)

The Jewish authorities want to stone Jesus because He claimed to pre-exist Abraham. Furthermore, His claim is to being divine when He uses the "I Am who I AM" which God identified Himself to Moses from the burning bush (Exodus 3:14). There is no doubt that the teachers and Priests of Judah recognize this as the title that God used when Moses asked God, who should I say sent me. They pick up stones to stone Jesus for blasphemy.

➢ **Peter:**

Peter is an Apostle who is with Jesus from the beginning of His ministry, through to the ascension of Jesus. He is a leader in the first century church growth and yet he stumbles frequently in his days with

Jesus. The biggest failure, being Peter's denial of knowing Jesus three times after the arrest of Jesus just, before Passover, in Jesus' third trip to Jerusalem. We see in all four books of the Apostles that Peter & John were early witnesses, to the discovery of the empty tomb. In John, we see the redemption of Peter, from his denial of Jesus in Jerusalem to the post resurrection appearances of Jesus finally in Galilee. After this event, the Apostles return to Jerusalem to wait for the coming of the Holy Spirit, which came at Pentecost, in Jerusalem. This event is captured in the first part of Acts by Luke. In it, Peter explains to the people who are gathered near the house where this occurs, wanting an explanation as to what has just happened. Peter tells them about what he knows about the Holy Spirit's coming and who Jesus really is in Acts 2:22-33,

> *22 "Fellow Israelites, listen to this: Jesus of Nazareth was a man accredited by God to you by miracles, wonders and signs, which God did among you through him, as you yourselves know. 23 This man was handed over to you by God's deliberate plan and foreknowledge; and you, with the help of wicked men, put him to death by nailing him to the cross. 24 But God raised him from the dead, freeing him from the agony of death, because it was impossible for death to keep its hold on him. 25 David said about him:*

> *"'I saw the Lord always before me. Because he is at my right hand, I will not be shaken. 26 Therefore my heart is glad and my tongue rejoices; my body also will rest in hope, 27 because you will not abandon me to the realm of the dead, you will not let your holy one see decay. 28 You have made known to me the paths of life; you will fill me with joy in your presence.'*

> *29 "Fellow Israelites, I can tell you confidently that the patriarch David died and was buried, and his tomb is here to this day. 30 But he was a prophet and knew that God had promised him on oath that he would place one of his descendants on his throne. 31 Seeing what was to come, he*

spoke of the resurrection of the Messiah, that he was not abandoned to the realm of the dead, nor did his body see decay. 32 God has raised this Jesus to life, and we are all witnesses of it. 33 Exalted to the right hand of God, he has received from the Father the promised Holy Spirit and has poured out what you now see and hear. (NIV)

Peter's testimony is that Jesus is the true Messiah, whom sinful men killed out of self-interest. However, God raised Jesus from the dead and that Peter and others have seen Him appear to them on several occasions. Peter knows and will testify to these facts.

Peter in his first letter to the church, recommends that believers must live exemplary lives of faith, because of the calling and salvation made by Jesus.

1 Peter 1:3-12

3 Praise be to the God and Father of our Lord Jesus Christ! In his great mercy he has given us new birth into a living hope through the resurrection of Jesus Christ from the dead, 4 and into an inheritance that can never perish, spoil or fade. This inheritance is kept in heaven for you, 5 who through faith are shielded by God's power until the coming of the salvation that is ready to be revealed in the last time. 6 In all this you greatly rejoice, though now for a little while you may have had to suffer grief in all kinds of trials. 7 These have come so that the proven genuineness of your faith—of greater worth than gold, which perishes even though refined by fire—may result in praise, glory and honor when Jesus Christ is revealed. 8 Though you have not seen him, you love him; and even though you do not see him now, you believe in him and are filled with an inexpressible and glorious joy, 9 for you are receiving the end result of your faith, the salvation of your souls. 10 Concerning this salvation, the prophets, who spoke of the grace that was to come to you, searched intently and with the greatest care, [11] trying to find out the time and circumstances to which the Spirit of Christ in them was pointing when he predicted the sufferings of the Messiah and the glories that would follow. [12] It was revealed to them that they were not serving themselves but you, when they spoke of the things that have now been told you by those who have preached the gospel to you by the Holy Spirit sent from heaven. Even angels long to look into these things. (NIV)

Peter reminds the church of Christ, which is growing rapidly, that it is because of Jesus and the work of redemption He has done on the cross, that their faith is effectual to save them. Furthermore, Peter has a surprising insight, that even the angels in heaven around God's throne are puzzled by this great work done by Jesus. Jesus, who now is in heaven, sitting at the right-hand of God, in the position of ultimate authority. Not only is this a position of authority on earth and in heaven but as we see in Hebrews 7:25-26, that Jesus now intercedes with the Father, for those who trusted Him.

[25] So he is able to save completely those who come to God through him, because he always lives to intercede for them. [26] For it is indeed fitting for us to have such a high priest: holy, innocent, undefiled, separate from sinners, and exalted above the heavens. (NIV)

We do not know who authored Hebrews, but it makes the same point that Peter makes that even now Jesus is at work in heaven, with His Father.

➢ **Paul:**

The testimony of Paul is astounding, given that he, as Saul, the persecutor of the Church of Christ, was recorded as being present at the first martyrdom recorded in the new testament church. Steven the Deacon to the Greek speaking church was martyred in Jerusalem for his speaking out about Jesus. Paul/Saul, who as a Pharisee, was a highly considered and was well educated Jew, living in Jerusalem. He encounters the resurrected Jesus on a trip to Damascus, with a warrant to seize any Jew who is a Jesus follower, living there. After this mystical confrontation, Jesus appoints Saul now called Paul to become the apostle to the gentiles.

In one of Paul's first letters to the church at Galatia, he is trying to correct an error that has come to affect the church that Paul and Barnabas planted there. He begins with a statement of foundational belief, to which Paul attests,

Galatians 1:1-5

> ^{1:1} *Paul, an apostle—sent not from men nor by a man, but by Jesus Christ and God the Father, who raised him from the dead—² and all the brothers and sisters with me, To the churches in Galatia: ³ Grace and peace to you from God our Father and the Lord Jesus Christ, ⁴ who gave himself for our sins to rescue us from the present evil age, according to the will of our God and Father, ⁵ to whom be glory for ever and ever. Amen.* ^(NIV)

Here is a persecutor of the church completely changed. He is spreading the fact that Jesus is alive and with His Father in heaven. He also attests to the fact that Jesus' death on the cross has rescued the faithful and justified those before God, into eternal life. Paul goes on from here, writing more than two thirds of the New Testament books. These books define the Doctrine of Justification by Faith, the doctrine of Christ's salvatory sacrifice, the doctrine of the final resurrection and the doctrine of Christ's imputed righteousness for believers. These are foundational to the universal church of Christ Jesus.

My Conclusion:

The scriptures in both the old and new testaments speak to the redemption of humanity. The coming of Jesus Christ is how we humans can be redeemed. Jesus sits in judgment today but also sits to intercede for His people at the same time. Only Jesus, fully God and fully man, can redeem and intercede for lost humanity.

Once again I am reminded that these books of the Bible were written by Forty different men over a period of 1500 years. They testify to the coming Messiah who could only be one person. My study of these many writers has lead me to recognize that Jesus of Nazareth is the "one" and "only person" that fits the description of the coming Messiah. What is even more compelling, is that if you go in search of the one true and living God, that search will bring you face to face with this Jesus. For me that realization opened up a relationship that progresses, as promised by Jesus to an everlasting and fulfilling eternity.

I am convinced that one of the greatest objections to the recognition of who Jesus Christ is that he came to this earth as a man. He began as an infant and grew to be a man, living in a small town in Palestine. He taught His disciples and taught in the great temple in Jerusalem. He never published anything and lived life as a carpenter, who at about thirty, became a traveling preacher at the crossroads of the trading routes between Africa, Asia and Europe. He was never recognized as a king until His death, sentence by Pilate. He was tried for blaspheme by the Jewish courts and never proved His guilt, although the Chief priest assumed he was guilty. He was tried by the Roman authority for treason and although Pilate pronounced Him innocent. He was sentenced to die by crucifixion.

However, we are told by his Apostles that Jesus lived a sinless. He died for our sins so that we could have peace with God the Father. He paid the penalty for the sins of the human race, who have been in rebellion to God ever since Adam & Eve were driven from the garden. God does not overlook sin. All sin must be paid for in order for us to be at peace with God. In the final analysis, man wants to stand before his judge in his own righteousness, but we are unable to do so even though we think we can.

PART 5

What does Jesus offer us today?

While many discount the bible because it is an ancient book, it has power and relevance for us today. I discovered this in my return to the teaching of Jesus when I was forty, in 1988. I found that it had relevant things to say about how I should live my life. It was relevant to my business life, family life, community life and church life.

The New Testament was written in Koine Greek which was the language of the Roman world at the turn of the first century. When I plumbed the depths of these 27 books, I found a surprising consistent testament from the writers and witnesses, as to what Jesus taught and did over the three years of His active teaching on earth. As we have seen in the previous section, Jesus did not hide His contention that He had come to earth from the Father in heaven. He taught us many concepts that are both radical and universal in today's technological world.

A. <u>What does Jesus offer us today?</u>

➢ <u>Peace, Rest, Contentment, and a cessation of war:</u>

In his teaching Jesus speaks of giving us peace, rest & contentment. In Matthew 11:28 Jesus says,

28 "Come to me, all you who are weary and burdened, and I will give you rest. (NIV)

This rest is Jesus taking over your burdens along with you as you walk in this life. Jesus is a burden carrier for those who are troubled. We do this in prayer and in the study of God's word which brings us perseverance for what may come upon us.

Just before he goes to the cross and His death Jesus tells his disciples, **_John 14:27 -28_**

"Peace I leave with you; my peace I give you. I do not give as the world gives. Do not let your hearts be troubled and do not be afraid. "(NIV)

By this Jesus is bestowing on His followers a personal peace and strength in times of fear and worry. Who in this world would not ask Jesus for some of that?

Jesus also talks about peace as a cessation of War. In *John 16:28-32*

29 Then Jesus' disciples said, "Now you are speaking clearly and without figures of speech. 30 Now we can see that you know all things and that you do not even need to have anyone ask you questions. This makes us believe that you came from God." 31 "Do you now believe?" Jesus replied. 32 "A time is coming and in fact has come when you will be scattered, each to your own home. You will leave me all alone. Yet I am not alone, for my Father is with me. 33 "I have told you these things, so that in me you may have peace. In this world you will have trouble. But take heart! I have overcome the world. "(NIV)

Here, Jesus is describing a change in the condition of the disciples. They were at war with God in their unbelief but now "in Me" you may have peace. This is the condition that occurs when a person puts their trust in Jesus to bring them into the Kingdom of God (or Kingdom of Heaven.)

In Luke 6: Jesus teaches about the wise and foolish builders. This parable is a word picture of what happens to people who listen to Jesus' teachings and follows them, versus the one who hears His teachings and ignores them.

Luke 6:46-49

46 "Why do you call me, 'Lord, Lord,' and do not do what I say? 47 As for everyone who comes to me and hears my words and puts them into practice, I will show you what they are like. 48 They are like a man building a house, who dug down deep and laid the foundation on rock. When a flood came, the torrent struck that house but could not shake it, because it was well built. 49 But the one who hears my words and does not put them into practice is like a man who built a house on the ground without a foundation. The moment the torrent struck that house, it collapsed and its destruction was complete."(NIV)

He is telling His listeners that there is an assured outcome for the person who is ready and willing to trust Jesus' words, then put them into practice, through trust. That outcome is a resilience to withstand difficulty and trials. In fact, He is offering peace in times when we are subject to the trials of life, whether they be family, health, occupational or neighbour issues, trust in Jesus will make us better able to live in peace.

➢ Love:

In his teachings on Love, Jesus does this in two ways. He speaks about how he loves us and how we should in turn, love our friends, family and enemies. This love is described in the Greek as "Agape" (love.) It is a love that is pure, unconditional and honourable in all ways.

{There are three word in Greek that describe love. The second being Phileo which is commonly described as brotherly love. It is affection or respect for others of our acquaintance who

have common interests. The third is Eros, which we equate to sexual love or attraction. Clearly, the highest form of Love is Agape}.

Jesus speaks about the Love that God the Father has for the Son of God. He tells His disciples that because Jesus has loved them, that the Father will love them too. In John 16:23-28 we see this outlined,

> *²³ In that day you will no longer ask me anything. Very truly I tell you, my Father will give you whatever you ask in my name. ²⁴ Until now you have not asked for anything in my name. Ask and you will receive, and your joy will be complete. ²⁵ "Though I have been speaking figuratively, a time is coming when I will no longer use this kind of language but will tell you plainly about my Father. ²⁶ In that day you will ask in my name. I am not saying that I will ask the Father on your behalf. ²⁷ No, the Father himself loves you because you have loved me and have believed that I came from God. ²⁸ I came from the Father and entered the world; now I am leaving the world and going back to the Father."*⁽ᴺᴵⱽ⁾

Through this relationship and love, God will hear and answer prayer for those who are in relationship with Jesus. For those with whom Jesus does not have a relationship, the prayer is not going to be heard. This rest is Jesus taking over your burdens along with you, as you walk in this life. Jesus is a burden carrier for those who are troubled.

Just before he goes to the cross and His death Jesus tells his disciples, John 14:27 -28,

> *"Peace I leave with you; my peace I give you. I do not give as the world gives. Do not let your hearts be troubled, nor let it be fearful.*⁽ᴺᴵⱽ⁾

Jesus is looking toward the crucifixion, which is but hours away, yet He tells His disciples that He is giving them His peace. It is a gift from Him that is not as the world gives but an empowerment that is supernatural. How is this possible given that in a matter of hours Jesus will be dead and buried in a sealed tomb. The answer to this is the offer that Jesus gives to everyone who trusts him. As His disciple John says, in John 1:11-13,

> *11 He came to that which was his own, but his own did not receive him.12 Yet to all who did receive him, to those who believed in his name, he gave the right to become children of God—13 children born not of natural descent, nor of human decision or a husband's will, but born of God.(NIV)*

This bestowed right of adoption into God's eternal family is what Jesus is talking about, that will give us supernatural peace, even in the face of death.

John 15:9-17

> *9 "As the Father has loved me, so have I loved you. Now remain in my love. 10 If you keep my commands, you will remain in my love, just as I have kept my Father's commands and remain in his love. 11 I have told you this so that my joy may be in you and that your joy may be complete. 12 My command is this: Love each other as I have loved you.13 Greater love has no one than this: to lay down one's life for one's friends. 14 You are my friends if you do what I command. 15 I no longer call you servants, because a servant does not know his master's business. Instead, I have called you friends, for everything that I learned from my Father I have made known to you. 16 You did not choose me, but I chose you and appointed you so that you might go and bear fruit—fruit that will last—and so that whatever you ask in my name the Father will give you. 17 This is my command: Love each other. (NIV)*

➢ Fellowship & Relationship:

In His teaching Jesus talks about having a personal relationship and fellowship with Him. How is this possible given that Jesus died and was buried? This is possible because Jesus is not now dead, nor in the grave, but He is alive and the tomb where Jesus was laid was found vacant on the Sunday morning. First, He speaks about how he loves us and how we should in turn love our friends, family and enemies. In 1 John 1:2-4, the Apostle John describes this fellowship, which is heavenly in nature,

> *² the life was made manifest, and we have seen it, and testify to it and proclaim to you the eternal life, which was with the Father and was made manifest to us—³ that which we have seen and heard we proclaim also to you, so that you too may have fellowship with us; and indeed our fellowship is with the Father and with his Son Jesus Christ. ⁴ And we are writing these things so that our joy may be complete. (ESV)*

John is talking about a lifetime fellowship that he understands both in the today and in the forever. The testimony is based on what he has witnessed in the life and times of Jesus Christ, but also in the life he has since experienced, in the growth and actions of the first century church of Christ. The same fellowship of believers is available today, for those who Trust in Jesus.

➢ Trust & Truth

Jesus teaches extensively about truth and belief or trust. What he says to the Jewish authorities is that they have put their trust in Abraham who is their father through lineage, but who is not their father in faith. He reminds them that Abraham trusted God to deliver him a son, well into his old age because God told him he would have a son who would be great. His trust in God justified Abraham before God. Now the Jewish authorities are confronted by Jesus, when He states that those who are His disciples both know the truth and are set free by that truth.

John 8:31-36

³¹ *To the Jews who had believed him, Jesus said, "If you hold to my teaching, you are really my disciples.³² Then you will know the truth, and the truth will set you free."*

³³ *They answered him, "We are Abraham's descendants and have never been slaves of anyone. How can you say that we shall be set free?"*

³⁴ *Jesus replied, "Very truly I tell you, everyone who sins is a slave to sin. ³⁵ Now a slave has no permanent place in the family, but a son belongs to it forever. ³⁶ So if the Son sets you free, you will be free indeed.* ^(NIV)

So, in discipleship in Jesus, there is understanding of truth and freedom from the penalties of the contamination of sin. The apostle John continues his witness of the teaching of Jesus in his letter to the first century churches. He speaks about how we should live as members of the churches of Christ. He is distinguishing between true believers and false believers of Christ. How can you make that distinction?

1 John 1:6-8

⁶ *If we claim to have fellowship with him and yet walk in the darkness, we lie and do not live out the truth. ⁷ But if we walk in the light, as he is in the light, we have fellowship with one another, and the blood of Jesus, his Son, purifies us from all sin. ⁸ If we claim to be without sin, we deceive ourselves and the truth is not in us.* ^(NIV)

The true believers will be evidenced by their walking in the light of Jesus teachings, which he points out, is truth.

➤ <u>Salvation:</u>

Those who trust Jesus do so because they understand that He came to earth to pay a heavy cost for the guilt (sin) burden that all humanity carries. We all stand before a righteous and holy God who has given us His laws as in the ten commandments and other pronouncements on our thinking and acting rightly before Him. We all stand guilty of some law breaking, because as Paul points out to the church in Rome,

Romans 1:18-25

[18] The wrath of God is being revealed from heaven against all the godlessness and wickedness of men who suppress the truth by their wickedness, [19] since what may be known about God is plain to them, because God has made it plain to them. [20] For since the creation of the world God's invisible qualities—his eternal power and divine nature—have been clearly seen, being understood from what has been made, so that men are without excuse. [21] For although they knew God, they neither glorified him as God nor gave thanks to him, but their thinking became futile and their foolish hearts were darkened. [22] Although they claimed to be wise, they became fools [23] and exchanged the glory of the immortal God for images made to look like mortal man and birds and animals and reptiles. [24] Therefore God gave them over in the sinful desires of their hearts to sexual impurity for the degrading of their bodies with one another. [25] They exchanged the truth of God for a lie and worshiped and served created things rather than the Creator—who is forever praised. Amen.[(NIV)]

The truth Paul is identifying is that the created world demonstrated the existence of God by the fact that it is there as opposed to nothing existing. If it exists and exists in its demonstrable designed complexity, then we should give God credit for existing and making what exists. Furthermore, we are also guilty before him of knowing the law because there is in each of us a guilt by association with our own conscience, which God has given us to know that there is an eternal and true law giver.

Now Jesus in His teaching of this says in **Matthew 12:36-38**,

> *36 But I tell you that everyone will have to give account on the day of judgment for every empty word they have spoken. 37 For by your words you will be acquitted, and by your words you will be condemned."(NIV)*

The bad news is that there is an accounting to be had for everyone who has ever lived. That accounting will be done using the evidence provided by our own words. Who of us has never spoken a word against God and His laws? Who of us can say that we have never thought murderous, covetous thievery or adulterous inclinations? We are all in need of forgiveness and salvation from our own thoughts as well as our deeds. In John 3:4, we see the words of Jesus to Nicodemus, a teacher of the law, who asked Jesus "how can a man be born again, when they are old?"(NIV) Jesus gives him the answer that is so profound that it can only be understood fully if we ask God to show us it is truth.

Jesus tells Nicodemus, a Teacher of the Law, that Salvation is from God. It is a free gift of God. It comes through faith when we trust that Jesus has paid for our guilt (sins), once for all. We can stand before a Holy and Just God in the truth that our own condemnation has been paid for by the Son of God.

In fact, Jesus spoke of this release from guilt when He promised his disciples that He was leaving them after His resurrection and He was going to heaven, in John 14:2,

> *2 My Father's house has many rooms; if that were not so, would I have told you that I am going there to prepare a place for you? (NIV)*

This promise is to all His disciples throughout time. Those who put their trust in Jesus and that He paid for their guilt & sin, will have eternal life with Him is heaven.

Elsewhere Jesus, the God man, offers humanity a gift of salvation. Unfortunately, this free gift is offered to everyone but not all will accept it. The reasons for rejecting this gift are many but all come down to the idea that I think I can do it for myself. Only those who discover that they are powerless to do it for themselves will be ready to accept the free gift of salvation through Christ Jesus. In Mark's gospel, he recalls the words of Jesus about how Jesus would ransom many through giving his life for them. In Mark 10: 42-45,

> *42 Jesus called them together and said, "You know that those who are regarded as rulers of the Gentiles lord it over them, and their high officials exercise authority over them. 43 Not so with you. Instead, whoever wants to become great among you must be your servant, 44 and whoever wants to be first must be slave of all. 45 For even the Son of Man did not come to be served, but to serve, and to give his life as a ransom for many." (NIV)*

Elsewhere John recalls Jesus words about this in John 10:14-18,

> *14 "I am the good shepherd; I know my sheep and my sheep know me—15 just as the Father knows me and I know the Father—and I lay down my life for the sheep. 16 I have other sheep that are not of this sheep pen. I must bring them also. They too will listen to my voice, and there shall be one flock and one shepherd. 17 The reason my Father loves me is that I lay down my life—only to take it up again. 18 No one takes it from me, but I lay it down of my own accord. I have authority to lay it down and authority to take it up again. This command I received from my Father." (NIV)*

Here Jesus makes the claim that He will lay down His life for the sheep of His pasture. Sheep He says that are His, given to Him by His Father, God. The stunning statement here is that Jesus has the power to lay down His life for His sheep, BUT He has the power and authority to take it up again. What Jesus is saying in the early part of His ministry in Judah, is that He knows He will die and rise again. It is through the resurrection that we know Jesus is not an ordinary man. He is the Son of God.

in John 5, Jesus, when confronted by the teachers of the law for healing people on the Sabbath day, replies in John 5:16-18,

> *16 So, because Jesus was doing these things on the Sabbath, the Jewish leaders began to persecute him. 17 In his defense Jesus said to them, "My Father is always at his work to this very day, and I too am working." 18 For this reason they tried all the more to kill him; not only was he breaking the Sabbath, but he was even calling God his own Father, making himself equal with God.* (NIV)

What the teachers took offense at was that Jesus admitted He was following God's own example, who though He ceased the creation on the seventh day, He continued to work in sustaining the creation and has done to ~~this~~ day. In this Jesus was identifying Himself with God the Father. Further on in John's gospel, Jesus discussed the relationship that He has with God the Father:

John 5: 19-27 The Authority of the Son

> *19 So Jesus said to them, "Truly, truly, I say to you, the Son can do nothing of his own accord, but only what he sees the Father doing. For whatever the Father does, that the Son does likewise. 20 For the Father loves the Son and shows him all that he himself is doing. And greater works than these will he show him, so that you may marvel. 21 For as the Father raises the dead and gives them life, so also the Son gives life to whom he will. 22 For the Father judges no one, but has given all judgment to the Son, 23 that all may honor the Son, just as they honor the Father. Whoever does not honor the Son does not honor the Father who sent him. 24 Truly, truly, I say to you, whoever hears my word and believes him who*

sent me has eternal life. He does not come into judgment, but has passed from death to life. 25 "Truly, truly, I say to you, an hour is coming, and is now here, when the dead will hear the voice of the Son of God, and those who hear will live. 26 For as the Father has life in himself, so he has granted the Son also to have life in himself. 27 And he has given him authority to execute judgment, because he is the Son of Man. (ESV)

These statements of Jesus are both encouraging and troubling. Jesus tells us that He has the power of the gift of Eternal Life. Salvation come though Faith in Him and His teaching. There is no other way than through Jesus because He has the authority of final judgment.

This is the first great impediment to people accepting the offer of salvation offered by Jesus. The idea that only Jesus and trust in His finished work, of paying for our guilt and sins, is the ONLY WAY, is somehow an anathema to people. Why is that, well because we somehow want there to be another way. But why would we want this. Because as Jesus says we are attracted to the darkness not the light of truth. In this day particularly we think there cannot be only one truth. However, if you discover that there is one creator, God over all in the cosmos, who has the power of truth and judgement, would you not be able to see that He and He alone will choose who will live with Him eternally? He sent His Son to pay your great debt of sin for you. A free gift that you must accept, as God has offers it. There is no negotiation with God.

There is a second great impediment to people accepting the salvation offered by Jesus. The second impediment is the near universal idea that somehow God will judge us on "the Curve". When you ask the man on the street, do you believe in life after death more that 70% say "yes". When asked how they will get into heaven, they generally say that they have done more good than bad, in their judgment.

What Jesus is saying, God does not judge on the "curve of some righteousness", but on the straight line of "Are you a law breaker of God's law"? If you have broken any one of God's laws, you are judged unworthy of heaven to live with God. There is only one man who has ever lived, who can say that He has not broken any laws of God. The man Jesus, can and does say that at His trial when confronted by Annas the father-in-law of the high priest Caiaphas, on the night of His arrest,

John 18:19-24,

19 Meanwhile, the high priest questioned Jesus about his disciples and his teaching. 20 "I have spoken openly to the world," Jesus replied. "I always taught in synagogues or at the temple, where all the Jews come together. I said nothing in secret. 21 Why question me? Ask those who heard me. Surely they know what I said."

22 When Jesus said this, one of the officials nearby slapped him in the face. "Is this the way you answer the high priest?" he demanded.

23 "If I said something wrong," Jesus replied, "testify as to what is wrong. But if I spoke the truth, why did you strike me?" 24 Then Annas sent him bound to Caiaphas the high priest. (NIV)

Jesus stands on all His teaching, all His public ministry and His whole life, was that He has broken no law, nor taught anything worthy of arrest. The writer of the book of Hebrews testifies further to this idea in Hebrews 4:14-16,

14 Therefore, since we have a great high priest who has ascended into heaven, Jesus the Son of God, let us hold firmly to the faith we profess. 15 For we do not have a high priest who is unable to empathize with our weaknesses, but we have one who has been tempted in every way, just as we are—yet he did not sin. 16 Let us then approach God's throne of grace with confidence, so that we may receive mercy and find grace to help us in our time of need. (NIV)

The one and only Son of God has come to save humanity. He has a righteousness that has been tried and proven. He is our High Priest in heaven, who intercedes for His people daily, before God.

➤ Life to the Full:

Jesus gives a promise that those who trust him, will live lives that are abundantly full in every way. He says in John 10:10,

> *¹⁰ The thief comes only to steal and kill and destroy; I have come that they may have life and have it to the full.*(NIV)

"By this he is saying that we will live lives that count in significant ways. We will live lives full of challenge and not lives that do not contribute. One writer, notes that …"*I am come that they might have life, and … more abundantly—not merely to preserve but impart LIFE AND communicate it in rich and unfailing exuberance. What a claim! Yet it is only an echo of all His teaching; and He who uttered these and like words must be either a blasphemer, all worthy of the death He died, or "God with us"—there can be no middle course.""³*

It is a life compared with that of someone lost and under the influence of the flesh, the world and Satan. That is a life of desperation that is ultimately insignificant by it lacking a central purpose. Jesus speaks about the abundance of the life He offers us. In Luke 6:37-38 when talking about judgement and the benefits of forgiveness.

> *³⁷ "Do not judge, and you will not be judged. Do not condemn, and you will not be condemned. Forgive, and you will be forgiven. ³⁸ Give, and it will be given to you. A good measure, pressed down, shaken together and running over, will be poured into your lap. For with the measure you use, it will be measured to you."*(NIV)

---

³ Jamieson, R., Fausset, A. R., & Brown, D. (1997). *Commentary Critical and Explanatory on the Whole Bible* (Vol. 2, p. 147). Oak Harbor, WA: Logos Research Systems, Inc.

The forgiving person will live this significant life in Jesus' authority. The forgiven life is one overflowing in forgiveness and godliness.

In John 17 before Jesus goes to the cross, He prays for the believers to come,

John 17:6-12,

6 "I have revealed you to those whom you gave me out of the world. They were yours; you gave them to me and they have obeyed your word. 7 Now they know that everything you have given me comes from you. 8 For I gave them the words you gave me and they accepted them. They knew with certainty that I came from you, and they believed that you sent me. 9 I pray for them. I am not praying for the world, but for those you have given me, for they are yours. 10 All I have is yours, and all you have is mine. And glory has come to me through them. 11 I will remain in the world no longer, but they are still in the world, and I am coming to you. Holy Father protect them by the power of your name, the name you gave me, so that they may be one as we are one. 12 While I was with them, I protected them and kept them safe by that name you gave me. None has been lost except the one doomed to destruction so that Scripture would be fulfilled. (NIV)

Jesus prays for our protection and perseverance. He prays that we will be one, together in spirit and truth, by the power of the Holy Spirit who enables us to live the abundant/significant life.

➤ Forgiveness and Justification:

As we have already seen above, Jesus offers us forgiveness. In Luke 7:43-58 Jesus reprimands a Pharisee who is thinking evil thoughts about a woman who has come into the Pharisee's house and poured her tears on Jesus' feet as an act of contrition.

⁴³ Simon replied, "I suppose the one who had the bigger debt forgiven." "You have judged correctly," Jesus said.

⁴⁴ Then he turned toward the woman and said to Simon, "Do you see this woman? I came into your house. You did not give me any water for my feet, but she wet my feet with her tears and wiped them with her hair. ⁴⁵ You did not give me a kiss, but this woman, from the time I entered, has not stopped kissing my feet. ⁴⁶ You did not put oil on my head, but she has poured perfume on my feet. ⁴⁷ Therefore, I tell you, her many sins have been forgiven—as her great love has shown. But whoever has been forgiven little loves little."

⁴⁸ Then Jesus said to her, "Your sins are forgiven."

⁴⁹ The other guests began to say among themselves, "Who is this who even forgives sins?" ⁵⁰ Jesus said to the woman, "Your faith has saved you; go in peace." ⁽ᴺᴵⱽ⁾

The Pharisee can only see the woman for her sins, but Jesus sees a woman wanting forgiveness of God. He asks the basic question that goes to the heart of everyone. Who will love greater, the one forgiven little or the one forgiven a great deal? Simon, the Pharisee, sees only her sin but is blind to the extent of his own sin. The conclusion that Jesus has for Simon and for all of us is, we all have a need for forgiveness. God is forgiving, but only of His own children.

Peter in his first letter to the church, 1 Peter 3:18 declares that Jesus gave us righteousness by suffering for our sins.

¹⁸ For Christ also suffered once for sins, the righteous for the unrighteous, to bring you to God. He was put to death in the body but made alive in the Spirit. ⁽ᴺᴵⱽ⁾

His suffering brought us life eternal and salvation though His death.

➤ Identity:

Those who come to Jesus and seek God "in Him" will be called Children of God.

John 1:11-13

¹¹ He came to that which was his own, but his own did not receive him. ¹² Yet to all who did receive him, to those who believed in his name, he gave the right to become children of God—¹³ children born not of natural descent, nor of human decision or a husband's will, but born of God.(NIV)

Through faith in Christ Jesus, we are being adopted into the Family of God. It is a permanent relationship that is based on the fellowship with the God in life now and in eternal life. It is founded upon the proposition, that you have been chosen by God into the fellowship and sealed with the Holy Spirit, so that your identity is with Christ is eternal.

Ephesians 1:13-14

¹³ In him you also, when you heard the word of truth, the gospel of your salvation, and believed in him, were sealed with the promised Holy Spirit, ¹⁴ who is the guarantee of our inheritance until we acquire possession of it, to the praise of his glory. (ESV)

"Identification is at the heart of the incarnation. As God became Man in Jesus, He was no Whitehall or Pentagon chief, making quick flying inspections of the front line, but one who shared the foxholes, who knew the risks, who felt the enemy fire. No other God has wounds. It is because God identified so fully with us that we know him and can trust Him." [4]

---

[4] Guinness, Os. (1973). <u>The Dust of Death</u>. InterVarsity Press (p. 387). Downers Grove, Illinois: 60515.

In Jesus, we have an intermediary who knows what being a human is completely like. He identifies with us and we have identity in Him, as an adopted Child of God's family forever.

➤ Assistance:

Jesus, when He was preparing for His crucifixion, told His disciples that He was leaving to return to the Father, but that He would not leave them alone. In John 14:7-11,

> *7 But very truly I tell you, it is for your good that I am going away. Unless I go away, the Advocate will not come to you; but if I go, I will send him to you. 8 When he comes, he will prove the world to be in the wrong about sin and righteousness and judgment:9 about sin, because people do not believe in me; 10 about righteousness, because I am going to the Father, where you can see me no longer;11 and about judgment, because the prince of this world now stands condemned.* (NIV)

Here we see that Jesus is referencing that He will send the Holy Spirit to the disciples. They are to listen to Him and follow His instructions. Jesus goes on to say that the Holy Spirit will provide them with Truth to live by. They should obey His leading. He also reminds them that the Holy Spirit will provide assistance that they need to live a Holy and upright life.

John 14:15-21

> *15 "If you love me, keep my commands. 16 And I will ask the Father, and he will give you another advocate to help you and be with you forever—17 the Spirit of truth. The world cannot accept him, because it neither sees him nor knows him. But you know him, for he lives with you and will be in you. 18 I will not leave you as orphans; I will come to you. 19 Before long, the world will not see me anymore, but you will see me. Because I live, you also will live. 20 On that day you will realize that I am in my Father, and you are in me, and*

I am in you. ²¹ Whoever has my commands and keeps them is the one who loves me. The one who loves me will be loved by my Father, and I too will love them and show myself to them."(NIV)

He will also remind the disciples that the Spirit will teach them and remind them of the things Jesus said and did.

John 14:25-27

²⁵ "All this I have spoken while still with you. ²⁶ But the Advocate, the Holy Spirit, whom the Father will send in my name, will teach you all things and will remind you of everything I have said to you. ²⁷ Peace I leave with you; my peace I give you. I do not give to you as the world gives. Do not let your hearts be troubled and do not be afraid. (NIV)

The Apostle Paul reminds us in Romans 8:26-30 that the Holy Spirit will lead and intercede for us,

²⁶ In the same way, the Spirit helps us in our weakness. We do not know what we ought to pray for, but the Spirit himself intercedes for us through wordless groans. ²⁷ And he who searches our hearts knows the mind of the Spirit, because the Spirit intercedes for God's people in accordance with the will of God. ²⁸ And we know that in all things God works for the good of those who love him, who have been called according to his purpose. ²⁹ For those God foreknew he also predestined to be conformed to the image of his Son, that he might be the firstborn among many brothers and sisters. ³⁰ And those he predestined, he also called; those he called, he also justified; those he justified, he also glorified. (NIV)

The Assistance in determining what we need most, is provided for by the Spirit of God.

➢ Grace:

There are several statements in the dictionary about what the qualities of grace are. Some refer to physical properties that enhance beauty or movement. Some definitions speak about embellishments to sound or music, which improve the song or speech. But the grace I want to focus on here, is the idea of favour. Benignant regard or manifestation of a superior to the lessor. In other words, receiving something which is not due to you, but is goodness when you do not deserve it. The apostle John quoting from John the Baptist says Jesus offers us grace in understanding God and His law more completely,

John 1:16-18

¹⁶ Out of his fullness we have all received grace in place of grace already given. ¹⁷ For the law was given through Moses; grace and truth came through Jesus Christ. ¹⁸ No one has ever seen God, but the one and only Son, who is himself God and is in closest relationship with the Father, has made him known. (NIV)

Both John & John the Baptist taught us that Jesus knows God intimately and if we enter into relationship with Jesus, we will know God and His law directly through what Jesus provides to us. He is referring to the Holy Spirit, which will indwell us.

The greatest grace gift that Jesus provides for us is outlined by the Apostle Paul in his letter to the church in Rome. In Romans 5:

⁶ You see, at just the right time, when we were still powerless, Christ died for the ungodly. ⁷ Very rarely will anyone die for a righteous person, though for a good person someone might possibly dare to die. ⁸ But God demonstrates his own love for us in this: While we were still sinners, Christ died for us. ⁹ Since we have now been justified by his blood, how much more shall we be saved from God's wrath through him! ¹⁰ For if, while we were God's enemies, we were reconciled to him through the death of his Son, how much more, having been reconciled, shall we be saved through his life! ¹¹ Not only is this so, but we also boast in God through our Lord Jesus Christ, through whom we have now received reconciliation. (NIV)

What greater grace gift could God offer to us, than even when we were sinners, an offense to God the Father, could Jesus His Son offer to us, than to die for our sins, thereby paying for the judgment of God of our sins, on our behalf. You are now and even in death, are entering into eternal life with Christ. This is the grace gift offered to humanity, that you can have forgiveness that erases the consequence of that sin. Further on in Romans 5:12-15;

¹² Therefore, just as sin entered the world through one man, and death through sin, and in this way death came to all people, because all sinned—¹³ To be sure, sin was in the world before the law was given, but sin is not charged against anyone's account where there is no law.¹⁴ Nevertheless, death reigned from the time of Adam to the time of Moses, even over those who did not sin by breaking a command, as did Adam, who is a pattern of the one to come. ¹⁵ But the gift is not like the trespass. For if the many died by the trespass of the one man, how much more did God's grace and the gift that came by the grace of the one man, Jesus Christ, overflow to the many! (NIV)

So, because we have accumulated our own lawless deeds and thoughts, we stand accused and guilty before God. But the Gift is given to undeserving sinners, that if they will accept it as offered, then they will have the grace of God over their future life. Forgiveness for all and an entitlement in the Son of God to eternal life with God.

➤ Assurance:

One of the final issues that Jesus gives to people today, is assurance. In John 5:24-25 Jesus says,

²⁴ "Very truly I tell you, whoever hears my word and believes him who sent me has eternal life and will not be judged but has crossed over from death to life. ²⁵ Very truly I tell you, a time is coming and has now come when the dead will hear the voice of the Son of God and those who hear will live. (NIV)*

Note here that Jesus does say that at that moment when you hear & believe that there is a transference that occur. You have moved from Death to Eternal life. This assurance is given in the present tense for a reason. It is because eternal life begins with this change. The currency of heaven is and always has been faith and not works. With faith comes assurance that though you will die, you have nothing to fear in death. You are now and even in death are entering into eternal life with Christ. I know that I am now living in the eternity to come by my faith in and promises of Christ Jesus. There is also an assurance that what Jesus says is true by the inescapable fact that the tomb of Christ was empty and that He appeared in bodily form to the following:

Resurrection appearances:		
A.	To Mary Magdalene	(John 20:11-17)
B.	To the Other women	(Matt. 28:9-10)
C.	To Peter	(1Corinthians 15:5
D.	To the disciples on the road to Emmaus	(Luke 24:13-35)
E.	To the Ten Disciple	(Luke 24:36-46)
F.	To the Eleven Disciple	(John 20:26-29)
G.	To the Seven Disciple at Galilee	(John 21:1-23)
H.	To more than five hundred	1 Corinthians 15:6)
I.	To the eleven at Ascension	(Matthew 28:16-20)

Furthermore, there is evidence that the tomb was empty by virtue of the story concocted by the Roman guards after sealing it with a Roman seal Then they posted guards at it. If the tomb was not empty and that all of the people who were convinced that He had risen, then the Romans and the Jewish authorities need only produce the body. No one has ever done this (i.e., produce the body).

The authorities never did because the Tomb was empty. One other point that needs recognizing here. The Romans soldiers were familiar with death. They broke the legs of the thieves on Jesus' right & left to hasten their deaths. Jesus was stabbed up through his side into the lungs & diaphragm which would have puncture the heart as well. This wound shows a discharge of blood and water which naturally occurs after death as the blood separates out and pools to the lowest extremities.

All of this should be an assurance that what is reported by eyewitnesses is true. Jesus did rise from the dead and is still alive. No one in the history of the world has done this. I consider this proof of life that Jesus is who He said he was, Jesus…Messiah, King of Kings, the Son of God, and my Saviour. He is worthy of trust and when you ask forgiveness for your guilt & sins, He will forgive you and make a guarantee of life with you which will extend into eternity. He will also begin a relationship that will only get better by the day.

➤ Knowledge of What God is like:

In several ways Jesus talks to his disciples to tell them what God the Father is like,

John 12:47-50

⁴⁷ Then Jesus cried out, "Whoever believes in me does not believe in me only, but in the one who sent me. ⁴⁵ The one who looks at me is seeing the one who sent me. ⁴⁶ I have come into the world as a light, so that no one who believes in me should stay in darkness. ⁴⁷ "If anyone hears my words but does not keep them, I do not judge that person. For I did not come to judge the world, but to save the world. ⁴⁸ There is a judge for the one who rejects me and does not accept my words; the very words I have spoken will condemn them at the last day. ⁴⁹ For I did not speak on my own, but the Father who sent me commanded me to say all that I have spoken. ⁵⁰ I know that his command leads to eternal life. So, whatever I say is just what the Father has told me to say."⁽ᴺᴵⱽ⁾

Jesus is teaching here in the Jerusalem temple, with many priests, scribes and Pharisees listening. He is telling them that what He teach teaches comes from God. They reject it at their peril, because it is straight from the Father through the Son, Jesus.

Later on, in the upper room Jesus is with His disciples and giving them His final instructions before he will be taken prisoner by the Sanhedrin, the chief priests and Pharisees. Jesus tells his disciples that he is going away and they need not worry because he will prepare a place for them. Thomas asks where you are going and why cannot we come…

John 14: 1-14

14:1 "Do not let your hearts be troubled. You believe in God; believe also in me. ² My Father's house has many rooms; if that were not so, would I have told you that I am going there to prepare a place for you? ³ And if I go and prepare a place for you, I will come back and take you to be with me that you also may be where I am. ⁴ You know the way to the place where I am going."

⁵ Thomas said to him, "Lord, we don't know where you are going, so how can we know the way?"

⁶ Jesus answered, "I am the way and the truth and the life. No one comes to the Father except through me. ⁷ If you really know me, you will know my Father as well. From now on, you do know him and have seen him."

⁸ Philip said, "Lord, show us the Father and that will be enough for us."

⁹ Jesus answered: "Don't you know me, Philip, even after I have been among you such a long time? Anyone who has seen me has seen the Father. How can you say, 'Show us the Father'? ¹⁰ Don't you believe that I am in the Father, and that the Father is in me? The words I say to you I do not speak on my own authority. Rather, it is the Father, living in me, who is doing his work. ¹¹ Believe me when I say that I am in the Father and the Father is in me; or at least believe on the evidence of the works themselves. ¹² Very truly I tell you, whoever believes in me will do the works I have been doing, and they will do even greater things than these, because I am going to the Father. ¹³ And I will do whatever you ask in my name, so that the Father may be glorified in the Son. ¹⁴ You may ask me for anything in my name, and I will do it⁽ᴺᴵⱽ⁾

So, Jesus is telling His disciples and all believers, that if they know and trust Jesus, they will know and trust God the Father because Jesus and the Father are one. Now this is a big thought that theologians have wrestled with for centuries. However, it is clear by what Jesus has said here and above, that if you know Jesus you also know God the Father.

This also goes one step further in that Jesus also says that He is sending a helper, the Holy Spirit who will indwell you and who will help us to live a victorious life in Christ.

John 14:15-21

¹⁵ "If you love me, keep my commands. ¹⁶ And I will ask the Father, and he will give you another advocate to help you and be with you forever—¹⁷ the Spirit of truth. The world cannot accept him, because it neither sees him nor knows him. But you know him, for he lives with you and will be in you. ¹⁸ I will not leave you as orphans; I will come to you. ¹⁹ Before long, the world will not see me anymore, but you will see me. Because I live, you also will live. ²⁰ On that day you will realize that I am in my Father, and you are in me, and I am in you. ²¹ Whoever has my commands and keeps them is the one who loves me. The one who loves me will be loved by my Father, and I too will love them and show myself to them."⁽ᴺᴵⱽ⁾

Elsewhere, Jesus tells his disciples that the Holy Spirit will remind them of what Jesus has said when they talk or write about Jesus. The promised Holy Spirit will also give specific gifts that are needed for the expansion of the Kingdom of God on earth, until Jesus returns again. Furthermore, Paul the apostle tells the Galatians church that the Holy Spirit will give us spiritual fruit that will help us overcome our fallen nature on a daily basis.

Galatians 5:16-26

> *[16] So I say, walk by the Spirit, and you will not gratify the desires of the flesh. [17] For the flesh desires what is contrary to the Spirit, and the Spirit what is contrary to the flesh. They are in conflict with each other, so that you are not to do whatever you want. [18] But if you are led by the Spirit, you are not under the law. [19] The acts of the flesh are obvious: sexual immorality, impurity and debauchery; [20] idolatry and witchcraft; hatred, discord, jealousy, fits of rage, selfish ambition, dissensions, factions [21] and envy; drunkenness, orgies, and the like. I warn you, as I did before, that those who live like this will not inherit the kingdom of God. [22] But the fruit of the Spirit is love, joy, peace, forbearance, kindness, goodness, faithfulness, [23] gentleness and self-control. Against such things there is no law. [24] Those who belong to Christ Jesus have crucified the flesh with its passions and desires. [25] Since we live by the Spirit, let us keep in step with the Spirit. [26] Let us not become conceited, provoking and envying each other.[(NIV)]*

Conclusion:

As for me, I have discovered these offers from the Son of God, both in the scriptures and in the living of my life. I know the presence of the Holy Spirit and understand my future is secure. Some have said to me how do you know for sure? What if you are wrong? I have said to them, that then I will have lived my life from 40 years of age on in the belief that I am blessed and destined for a heaven with God the Father, God the Son and the in-dwelling Holy Spirit in the optimistic idea of this "hope" that rules my life. Considering the opposite of Hope - Hopelessness which do you choose?

All this truth is compelling. However, the greatest idea that I invite you to consider is this: 'If you enter into relationship with this Jesus; He will accept you and will befriend you in a relationship that is unlike any friendship you have ever had. You will discover in this relationship that He will communicate with you through prayer, through the Word of God, through the Holy Spirit and through others who have a relationship with him. The big idea is you have the opportunity to become the friend of the Living God, which is beyond anything anyone has ever given you or ever will.'

John 15:12-17

12 My command is this: Love each other as I have loved you. 13 Greater love has no one than this: to lay down one's life for one's friends. 14 You are my friends if you do what I command. 15 I no longer call you servants, because a servant does not know his master's business. Instead, I have called you friends, for everything that I learned from my Father I have made known to you. 16 You did not choose me, but I chose you and appointed you so that you might go and bear fruit—fruit that will last—and so that whatever you ask in my name the Father will give you. 17 This is my command: Love each other. (NIV)

To be a friend of Jesus is to be a friend of God the Father. To be a friend of Jesus and God the Father is to possess the Holy Spirit, the seal of guaranteeing what is to come. (2 Corinthians 1:22) This is an invitation "to friend" that is far more significant than an on-line ephemeral "friending" you will ever encounter. The consequences are eternal from the moment you make it.

All you need do right now, is to ask Jesus to come into your life and be with you into eternity. Ask Him to forgive your faults and errors of your life, and he will forgive you as he has said in the scripture. He will send the Holy Spirit to you to make you compatible with the Father for the rest of your life. At this point if you have done this it is best to tell someone that you have prayed to receive Christ and look for people who will help you understand the full implication of this mysterious change in your life.

PART 6

What happens when we die?

There are many ideas as to what comes after death. What is interesting is that throughout all cultures on earth there is an expectation of life after death. The only cultural group who disagree, are the true atheists who say that there is nothing after death. They are required to say that, because the logical conclusion is that if there is no God, then there cannot be anything supernaturally occurring after death. However, I think that idea is unworkable as a philosophy of life because it will make us into people who live only for today. Ultimately, this idea will drive you into seeing futility in life. If there is no life after death, then why am I here? Am I just a pleasure machine? Life after death goes to the deepest understanding of what is the meaning of life.

A. <u>What about the Jewish idea of After life?</u>

The Jewish believers accept that God, an infinite being who exists and created all things, will judge every man at his death. The Jewish believer understands that life of man does not begin with birth, but rather with conception. At conception, man is a body and soul unity. The Jewish believers understand that the body and soul are separated at death.

The believer will be judged righteous if he has lived by the Laws of God (Torah) and understands the full meaning of what is meant by God's given Laws (Talmud- a commentary of writings from 300AD and beyond, on the Laws and Prophets). In Jewish understanding the keeping of the Law and understanding of the Law is a practiced life of actions. This keeping the law is the ultimate purpose of life. Those who succeed in keeping the Law will be rewarded in death. Those who have not succeeded, will be punished in death. The idea of being in the company of your ancestors Abraham, Isaac & Jacob is more of the Jewish idea of heaven, than living in the presence of God. Those who were not judged to be law keepers were destined to a solitary existence without ancestors, in a place called Gehenna or Guion. It is often described as a deep dark pit.

The Torah (first Five Books of the Bible) is largely silent upon the subject of heaven & hell; however, tradition allows for a division of people who trust God and keep the law versus those who flaunt the law of God. Jesus, when asked about this, tells a story of two men going to the afterlife. He describes it as separation that is insurmountable between those judged good, living with Father Abraham and those judged undeserving, left out in a place of torment.

The process of mourning in Jewish households can last eleven months after death. Kaddish is a prayer said for the deceased. It is repeated in order to protect the dignity & merit of the individual who died before God. Orthodox Judaism believes that prior to a soul's entry into heaven some mourners are to say "Kaddish", over that period, for the deceased. There is an understanding of a better place in some Talmud writings, so called Gan Eden or heaven. This is harking back to a place of peace, joy, and celebration in this concept. There is a division between some, as to whether there will be a resurrection of the body or no resurrection, but just a spiritual existence. Those who expect the resurrection, assume it to correspond to the coming of the Messiah.

B. What about animists believe about the afterlife?

First, Animism is the typical belief system of Indigenous peoples all over the world, who hold that there is an aspect of spirit life in most things, be they animals, trees, rivers or seas. This world view often is represented as spirit from the past generations of each item, which holds some influence over the current situation that is evident today. This then will see current people groups as being a continuance of the past generations and see death as merely a continuation of what is today, only in a Spirit form.

From this idea comes the expectation, that you can appeal to the ancestors to control the current situation today. This often will encourage Shamanism to help those who are alive today to appeal to the ancestral spirits of the past to help with today. Animists would see that after death, comes a spiritual existence, that to a certain extent can have power that will affect the happenings today. This is not pantheism, as there is a clear understanding that the spirits exist individually, distinct from one another.

C. What about the Christian's idea of After life?

In Christianity, there is solid agreement for the existence of life after death. Furthermore, there is widespread agreement that death is a separation of the soul and body, or in some cases, a separation of the soul & Spirit from the body at death. The Christian idea of death is that the separation is a "Spiritual" separation of the body, with its physical form, from the nonphysical (Soul or Soul & Spirit). According to Christian understanding, man is not just physical, but is physical body and soul from conception. Death is understood to be the separation of the nonphysical from the physical, which is understood to be temporary. Man is seen to be a soul with a physical body, with the soul/spirit existing forever. The question is, where.

Resurrection is understood to be a physical resurrection, sometime in the future, in which those who have died, believers and nonbelievers, are resurrected with a physical body, to live with this body, in eternity. The resurrection occurs with the Second Coming of Christ Jesus to earth.

The question that haunts this resurrection is where you will spend your eternal life in the new body?

Judgment is rendered as to whether you are destined for eternal life with God or eternal life without God. The deciding factor is whether you have a relationship in this life with Christ Jesus or whether you do not have a relationship with Christ Jesus.

Heaven - Those who have accepted Jesus offer to have his death pay for their sins and thereby enter into a relationship with Christ Jesus, receive the Holy Spirit, which is a seal, giving covenantial assurance of their eternity with God. This existence is both spiritual and physical after the resurrection.

Hell - Those who have rejected the offer of Jesus' salvation, will live out their resurrection in Hell. The original purpose for Hell was that it is a place that was designed to contain the demons & Satan. Those who are destined for hell, will live in eternity in separation from God, because of their choices in this life, to rebuff the free gift of salvation, offered by Jesus Christ. There is no chance for change of destiny once death comes.

Roman Catholics believe there is still a need to pay for the sins one has committed in this life, once you are dead. They call this "purgatory". They believe there is a need to pay for unconfessed sins done before death, for people who are in need of purification, to enter heaven. This idea was part of the cause of a split between the Orthodox and Protestant churches over the centuries. The idea of Purgatory come from the Second Council of Lyon 1272 & 1274 under Pope Gregory X. The rejection by Orthodox & Protestant churches is based upon the concept of "Sola Christos", Latin for "Christ alone" which means only Christ Jesus' death is necessary to pay for your sins. There is no need for purging of sins in some holding area, between heaven and hell.

The concept is that when Jesus died on the cross, His last statement was "it is finished". He uses a term *"tetelestai"* in the Greek which is an accounting or trade term which means "paid in full". The idea of Purgatory goes against this idea. However, if we take Jesus at His word, then we can know that the moment when we accept His offer of forgiveness and exchanged His life and death, to pay for our sin life, is the moment in our lives, where we gain justification before a Holy God, with total forgiveness. In fact, our sins are removed from us as far as the "east is from the west".

One of the essentials of Christianity is the Death of Jesus Christ on the cross. It is foretold in Isaiah 53; Psalm 22; Daniel 9:26; Amos 8:9 and Zechariah 11:10-13 in several ways, that the Messiah would be betrayed, tried and killed. Many of these prophetic utterances specify the amount of the bribe for Judas, and that Jesus would be subjected to the piercing of Jesus hands and feet. Several specifics are startling, right down to the gambling for Jesus' clothing at the foot of the cross, to the fact His body would be entombed in a borrowed grave of a rich man. The essential question though is, "Why did Jesus die?" He was an innocent man who lived with the fullness of obedience to the Law. He became our sin debt payment, which was applicable for anyone who wished to accept God's offer of forgiveness and righteousness.

Romans 3:25-26

> [25] *God presented Christ as a sacrifice of atonement, through the shedding of his blood—to be received by faith. He did this to demonstrate his righteousness, because in his forbearance he had left the sins committed beforehand unpunished—[26] he did it to demonstrate his righteousness at the present time, so as to be just and the one who justifies those who have faith in Jesus.* (NIV)

Now this essential is different from all religions of the world. God is here-by offering His Son to provide a ransom that pays for our lawlessness and also that provides a credit of righteousness to the lawbreaker, who has no way of being counted as righteous. However, Jesus lived a perfect life abiding by All of God's laws. His righteousness is applied to cover our unrighteousness, when Christ paid our penalty. When we appear before God at the final judgment, those who are in fellowship with Jesus Christ, through trust placed in Him and His death sacrifice, before death are judged righteous by God, because of our union with Jesus. This union with Christ is the result of Faith. Faith that His sacrifice will be effective in paying for our many sins. Trust that Jesus perfect sinless life provides us with His righteousness – borrowed and imputed to us.

My Conclusion:

I have come to believe that the Christian world view is more reasonable, than each of these other ideas about the afterlife. To me there is solid evidence in scripture, that the teaching of Jesus offers me hope and grace, which is going to see me safely into the next life. I believe that an anticipation of life after death is certain, when I consider how widespread this concept is throughout all cultures. Furthermore, the idea that there will be a judgment seems rational, given that most worldviews are prepared to recognize a system of good versus evil behaviors, which is specific to all cultures over all time. (Ten commandment type ideals).

I have investigated these truths and there is much to substantiate that Jesus did rise from the dead. The offer he makes to all humanity is that His teachings have supernatural power. His offer of eternal life is both logical and substantial.

So, for me to stand in the "Great Assizes in judgment before a Holy All-knowing God" to give my justification, seems to be highly risky. I can avoid this by accepting Jesus as my Saviour, knowing that His righteousness is more than adequate to cover me, while for me to hope in a weighed scale of good verses bad, is in the order of the law of karma where no one is certain ever. This I have done and recommend that you do the same. All you need do is pray that the truth of what Jesus has done for you would become clear to you. Go then and join with others who have made that commitment, then see how your life and future will change for the better.

Furthermore, the concept of hell as a distinct and permanent destination for unbelievers, makes sense to me. People who have rejected God, His offer of forgiveness and mercy, are people who never wanted God in their lives. Their independent lives, free from God's apparent control and obligations, would only be a further burden on them in the afterlife. As one writer has put it "the gates of hell are firmly locked from the inside", not the outside.

Furthermore, to hope that a Holy God who has demonstrated that ALL sin must be paid, whether the smallest prevarication to the greatest murder, is a daunting idea. We can say I am sorry so many times, but it is pay day some day for all of us. People who think God is a nice old man who looks like George Burns living in heaven are deceived.

Furthermore, when it comes to death, all the teachers of the world religions are dead and long gone, except ONE. At His Death there was a large audience of witnesses, the Jewish authorities a Roman Centurion and Roman guard, The Roman centurion who has had a substantial experience in death will confirm to Governor Pontius Pilate that Jesus was dead. The death and resurrection of Jesus is an essential of Christianity. Historically there are many references to the fact that the tomb was empty. His burial was witnessed by Joseph of Arimathea & Nicodemus (John 19:38-42) who did the burial in a tomb belonging to Joseph. It was witnessed by Mary Magdalene, Mary the mother of Joses, Joanna, Mary the mother of James(Matthew 27:61; Mark 15:47; Luke 24:10;).

Notwithstanding all of the above, there is substantial evidence that on the morning of the third day, Sunday, the women went to anoint the body of Jesus. They were the second ones to discover the stone covering the tomb entrance was rolled away and tomb was empty. The first to determine that it was empty were the Roman guards who had been posted by Pilate & the Jewish High Priest to prevent any disturbance of the tomb. The Roman guards were witness to the tomb being opened up supernaturally. The Roman guard who were war hardened men, would do their duty or face the death penalty. They had abandoned their charge of guarding the tomb of a Jewish teacher, the body of Jesus. They experienced something so great that they fainted in fright, then ran away.

The essential to the faith of Christians, is that Jesus rose again from the dead on the third day, to underline the fact that He and only He, had overcome death. This then becomes the truth that uniquely stands as different from all other world religions. Jesus promised, through His resurrection, to bring all who believe, into the afterlife with the assurance of SALVATION unto an eternity with God.

PART 7

Why Is there Evil in the World?

First the idea that evil exists assumes that there is also "Good". Without being able to differentiate "good" from "evil", means that both must exist, and both must be recognizable by some predetermined values or concepts. Good and Evil are only possible, if God exists. Good and Evil must be determined by One Being, who is able to determine good and evil by valuation within His authority. If you use any other concept for "Good" & "Evil", you will come to a community standard that changes over time, then is subject to change, often without notice.

> **Why must Good and Evil transcend cultural or situational boundaries:**

Without an unchangeable valuation for Good and Evil we will never be able to judge what is evil or good. If they (good & evil) can be changed at the will of the defendant before the judge or at the will of the judge, then justice is never going to be achieved. As a society we can make rules, but when one government leaves and a new one comes in, the laws will change. Does the concept of Evil and Good change with those laws? If they do change, then we can be doing evil on day one but declared having done good on the very next day after passing new laws. We have seen this happen over many times in history, the defense that "I was just following orders," has been tested and found wanting.

> ## Why does Evil Exists:

The problem of evil is an issue for every type of philosophy. If I come into an atheist's office and steal his computer, he may object, but if there is no outside moral law that is the same for everyone for all time; his objections would have no sound basis. All I need to plead is that it may be evil in his mind but in my mind what is his, is mine and it is good because I have a computer now. After all isn't "From each according to his ability; to each according to his need" a principle set down by Karl Marx.

> ## How do different Religions deal with Evil?

For all religions, humanity operated in a world of will or volition. We know what we want to do and can think of ways of do it. However, we have in our volition, a sense of ought and ought not. This is the extension and outward signs of conscience. Furthermore, when we consider what we want, there is a balancing act going on conceptually, whereby we consider the what, the how and the why of our want. This is what we know as rational thought. Rational thought is a metaphysical concept (relating to the part of philosophy that is about understanding, existence and knowledge). We may consider our "gut feelings," but this is not a sign of stomach problems. Nor is the desire of affections, a feeling somewhere in your underwear. These are metaphysical ideas that are not based in the physical & material parts of man.

Jewish concept of man:

In Jewish concept of Man views, man is both spirit (Soul) and material (body). The spiritual side of man and the physical side of man both need to be redeemed from the power of sin and death. The original genesis of man was in a dual formation which God considered "it very Good" (NIV) (Genesis 1:31). It was only after the fall of man in Genesis 3 that man's physical and spiritual condition changed. That we are made up of body and soul is indicated in the creation account:

Genesis 2:7

"And the Lord God formed man from the dust of the ground, and breathed into his nostrils the breath of life, and man became a living soul" (NIV).

In the creation imagery, man's body is formed first. But the body without the soul remains lifeless. When God breathes the breath of life into the body, then man becomes a living soul. God creates the soul and the body. It is determined that the soul survives death because God specifically created it. Death comes to the body in the fall but the soul remains. It survives the death because it is sustained and preserved by the power of God.

Matthew10:28

The soul of man can live without the body; the body cannot live without the soul. Jesus exhorted His hearers: "Do not be afraid of those who kill the body but cannot kill the soul. Rather, be afraid of the one who can destroy both the soul and the body in hell" (NIV)

From this biblical revelation we know we have souls. The Bible does not banish the soul to some lost in space idea of atheism. We have souls which will outlast the current bodies on earth. Based on this idea the care and nurturing of our souls is seen as a central focus of the Christian life.

Christianity:

From the Jewish concept of man, Christians derive their understanding of humanity. In the Westminster Confession of Faith, we are told that man was made by God and endowed with knowledge, righteousness and true holiness after His own image. Implied in the formation of man by God is

123

that man was first created then woman created second as a help mate and one who was to have fellowship with man.

> *After God had made all the other creatures, he created man, male and female, [4] with reasoning, immortal souls. [5]He endowed them with knowledge, righteousness, and true holiness in his own image [6] and wrote his law in their hearts. [7]God also gave them the ability to obey his law and the potential to disobey it, i.e., he gave them freedom of their own will, which could change. [8] In addition to this law written in their hearts, they were commanded not to eat from the Tree of the Knowledge of Good and Evil. [9] As long as they obeyed God's law and kept this commandment, they were happy in fellowship with God[10] and had dominion over the other creatures.*

(Westminster Confession of Faith, pp10).

From the Bible, Christians understand that man was made different from all the other beings on earth because man was made "in the image of God". Now that does not imply that man was divine, but rather that man was a thinking (rational) being, that comprised more than just a physical body. God made man, who is a physical being, with an ability to relate to God on a spiritual basis. We see this in the creation story as God walked with Adam in the cool of the evening. This is a relationship of rich communion, man being physical having a spiritual & intellectual relationship to the transcendent God. The relationship between man and God is one of a covenant relationship where God in his grace has made everything on earth and then delegated it to man's "dominion". He gives man the right to name the animals and to work the garden in what was to be a prefect fellowship relationship between man and God.

The only condition God gives man, is that he is not eat of the tree of the knowledge of good and evil. This is what, in classical theology is called a "Covenant of Works". God being the greater authority by virtue of creation, out of His grace gives man a purpose that also comes with a condition. The purpose is to work the garden and to fellowship with his God. God gives this purpose, creating man with soul, will and body. We are told that God created man "very good" (Genesis 1:31) and God then sees that man is lacking something and He creates two things for Adam. First He creates "Eve" as a helper because he was alone. Second God institutes the covenant of marriage and the institution of the family. These are the foundational institutions of culture and civilization.

Genesis 1:24

> *²⁴ That is why a man leaves his father and mother and is united to his wife, and they become one flesh. ²⁵ Adam and his wife were both naked, and they felt no shame. (NIV)*

The one condition was that defined by Genesis 2:15-16,

> *¹⁵ The LORD God took the man and put him in the Garden of Eden to work it and take care of it. ¹⁶ And the LORD God commanded the man, "You are free to eat from any tree in the garden; ¹⁷ but you must not eat from the tree of the knowledge of good and evil, for when you eat from it you will certainly die." (NIV)*

So, Adam and Eve are given this one imperative that they not eat of the tree of "good" and "evil", with the warning of when you eat of it you will surely die. The first family of our family tree had really only one commandment, which came with a dire warning. Many people say "Why would God give them this warming if they had such an idyllic life, where only "Very Good" would be their lives? The answer to this is, God is a loving and righteous God. His offer to Adam & Eve was one in which they could choose God and a life of relationship and blessing with him, or they could choose their own path in rebellion, to Him. Unfortunately, they chose the rebellion, by the tempter's words "you will be like God, knowing good and evil. This idea seemed like it would give them something they already had, being like God. However, it was against the one imperative that God had given them the only thing they should not do.

Genesis 2:15

¹⁵ The Lord God took the man and put him in the Garden of Eden to work it and take care of it. ¹⁶And the Lord God commanded the man, "You are free to eat from any tree in the garden; ¹⁷ but you must not eat from the tree of the knowledge of good and evil, for when you eat from it you will certainly die."⁽ᴺᴵⱽ⁾

From this act of rebellion came the fall of man and into the world came two serious conditions that affected the whole earth. The first was evil. Until this event humanity only knew good. Now he had the knowledge of both GOOD and EVIL. The second event was death came to humanity and the whole earth. There is substantial proof for these things being true as told from the beginnings of the Bible. There is nothing on earth to this day that is not subject to death…nothing.

The first is the idea of evil. Man, at the fall became one who is solely concerned first for himself over all others. He may have a conscience, but his selfishness often outweighs the selfless path. He measures everything by his own benefit first before any other consideration. In fact, when you ask anyone on the street, "Why they would expect that they deserved heaven?" What is their normal answer? "I think my good deeds outweigh my bad." However, we know now that we are not an unbiased judge of ourselves. We are a fallen judge, with a bias to judge our own deeds by what seems good to us, over anyone else.

Surely God would not hold us responsible for what our first parents did. Why yes, He does because we are now affected with the illness of selfishness that came upon our father Adam. It has affected the whole of humanity in our genetics, thought life and motives. We have lost the ability to seek God on our own and the ability to hear Him. What we need is an opening of our heart to a new way of thinking that seeks God. What we need is to want a relationship with God like our father Adam once had.

So why is there evil in the world? Because our forebearer choose rebellion over obedience to a loving and just God. We like Adam before us are now selfish and self-indulgent which is rebellion to God.

Conclusion:

BUT why doesn't God either change things or allow everyone who has made the error of selfishness to be forgiven. He has done exactly that, by offering up His own son Jesus of Nazareth, to do two things that we need desperately. The first is that we need someone who will save us from the chain of many sins that we have in our lives. Those sins can be paid in full. We are told, by the death of the perfect sacrifice of Jesus, whose life was totally sinless, without any selfishness or rebellion we can be redeemed. This payment of the blood of Jesus, does pay for every selfish or evil deed we have committed in our lives. The second thing we need is to be made righteous before God, because He will not allow unrighteousness into a relationship with Him. This righteousness too is offered by Jesus because His righteous life is offered to us as an imputed righteousness. When God looks upon someone who is "in" Christ Jesus, God forgives them. God also counts them as righteous just as Adam and Eve were before the fall.

For all religions, humanity operates in a world of will or volition. We know what we want to do and can think of ways to do what we want. What we need to be able to do is live according to God's good will, in cooperation with Him and in His word. There is only one way to do that, is to ask God to change you from a rebellious individual to one who seeks God.

PART 8

Are All religions the same idea just expressed differently?

There is a view that all religions are the same, just differing views based upon cultural ideas of truth. From this view there are several different ideas about God and man, but each one has only a piece of the real truth. It is much like the five blind men who encounter an elephant. One touches the trunk and says the elephant is round and long like a snake. The second one feels the tusk and says no it is hard and pointed like a stake. The third feels the ear and says no the elephant is like a piece of leather. The fourth feels the leg and says the elephant is like a tree. Finally, the fifth one feels the tail and says that the elephant is like a rope. Not one has a complete picture of the true elephant.

A. <u>God is perfect in Every Way.</u>

The God of Christianity is a perfect being. He has disclosed to us what is considered good and what is considered bad (sin) according to Him. We find these in the first five books of the Bible. His idea as disclosed therein, is that He is perfect and perfection is how He judges obedience. If you transgress any of these laws you are a sinner who must be redeemed. Remember that God being the creator of all things gives Him the right of ownership. He can do with anything whatever He likes because of His being the source of origin. However, He is trustworthy and good beyond our understanding of the term "Goodness."

B. <u>God is A Judge of Good and Bad Behaviour, Values and Ethics:</u>

The idea that God would consider all our good and bad deeds and then weigh them, to judge if we get into heaven, is based upon the idea of a works-based entitlement. Most organized religions are premised upon this concept – that your works good and bad count.

In the Hindu religion, their idea that my good deeds count against my bad deeds, is how Hindu's Karma principle works. There is a sense that each religion lays out what are good and what are bad works. Then the Cosmic judge will be governed by these rules. Unfortunately, these have been created by man, who is a biased judge.

For Islam and Judaism, as defined today, there is an expectation that your good works in this life as defined by their book and writers, count for your good by God. Even in Buddhism, the idea is that we can achieve Nirvana by doing the things that Buddha defined as good (the four Truths & Eight-way path). Only Nirvana is the arrival at a place where you no longer exist as an individual but have crossed over into the universal being.

C. <u>Sin must be paid for to be Mitigated Permanently.</u>

In the first Five books of the Bible Genesis, Exodus, Leviticus, Numbers and Deuteronomy, God sets out the laws of God. We get the moral law governing what is right and wrong here. Today we have much of this moral law written upon our conscience but the law giver has defined these lines of behaviour, in these five books.

God has also defined the ceremonial law that governed the Jews for 1600 years. The ceremonial law was given to recognize that all sin must be paid (moral law breaking). In the ceremonial law, several methods of covering over the law breaking, were given in the form of offerings and sacrifices. What we see in this, is the idea that through a sacrifice, you could restore your standing before your God. However, you were still known to God as a "sinner/law breaker". You sacrifice covered your sin; it did not erase it. What you needed was to be redeemed by a redeemer who had lived a perfect life, never having broken the law of God. The Ten Commandments are a good representation of the moral law. Jesus then adds condensed them to those the Golden rules in Matthew 22:34-38,

> ³⁴ *Hearing that Jesus had silenced the Sadducees, the Pharisees got together.* ³⁵ *One of them, an expert in the law, tested him with this question:* ³⁶ *"Teacher, which is the greatest commandment in the Law?"* ³⁷ *Jesus replied: "Love the Lord your God with all your heart and with all your soul and with all your mind.'* ³⁸ *This is the first and greatest commandment.* ³⁹ *And the second is like it: 'Love your neighbor as yourself.'* ⁴⁰ *All the Law and the Prophets hang on these two commandments."* (NIV)

The First four commandments are summarized in "Love your God with your heart, soul & mind" The second, "love your neighbour as yourself summarizes the last six commandments. The first according to Jesus is your required fidelity to God. Then he points to loving your neighbour as yourself. These are high measure fidelity to humanity.

D. <u>God sends a perfect Redeemer:</u>

God has provided for the redemption of the law breaker, who will pay for our sins after having lived upon the earth, a perfect law-abiding life. Jesus did this because He was born into this world without the fatal flaw that all humans have. We are self-centered and rebellious to the laws of God. No one can say to God, "I have perfectly kept your laws all of my life". God sent His own son, Jesus the Christ to live a life of perfect obedience to His laws, because Jesus loved His Father and He loved and knew the law perfectly.

<u>John 3:14-21</u>

> ¹⁴ *Just as Moses lifted up the snake in the wilderness, so the Son of Man must be lifted up,* ¹⁵ *that everyone who believes may have eternal life in him."* ¹⁶ *For God so loved the world*

that he gave his one and only Son, that whoever believes in him shall not perish but have eternal life. ¹⁷ For God did not send his Son into the world to condemn the world, but to save the world through him. ¹⁸ Whoever believes in him is not condemned, but whoever does not believe stands condemned already because they have not believed in the name of God's one and only Son. ¹⁹ This is the verdict: Light has come into the world, but people loved darkness instead of light because their deeds were evil. ²⁰ Everyone who does evil hates the light and will not come into the light for fear that their deeds will be exposed. ²¹ But whoever lives by the truth comes into the light, so that it may be seen plainly that what they have done has been done in the sight of God. ^(NIV)

This classic set of verses from the Gospel of John, one of Jesus' disciples, reveals that the way to eternal life is not doing good, but is trusting in the goodness of the Son of God. The idea here then, is that those who trust that God will be obligated to offer them heaven because of their good works, is trusting in the fatal flaw of darkness in the knowledge and actions of perfectly keeping God's law.

Paul and Silas who were imprisoned in Philippi, responded to their jailer, who after an earthquake feared that all his prisoners had escaped and he would be held accountable with his life. When he realized that this was sent to show him his vulnerability, he asked Paul what He must do to be saved...

Acts 3:31-33.

³¹ They replied, "Believe in the Lord Jesus, and you will be saved—you and your household." ³² Then they spoke the word of the Lord to him and to all the others in his house. ³³ At that hour of the night the jailer took them and washed their wounds; then immediately he and all his household were baptized.^(NIV)

Peter explains that what we needed was a perfect sacrifice to cover our sins…

1 Peter 3:18

[18] For Christ also suffered once for sins, the righteous for the unrighteous, to bring you to God. He was put to death in the body but made alive in the Spirit. (NIV)

The reason Jesus came to earth was to die for our sins. He was sent to destroy the works of the devil that cause man to fall into sin and death.

E. Assurance that I have eternal Life & forgiveness of Sins.

John the Apostle also confirms that once you have accepted the offer of salvation, your sins are all paid for before salvation and after salvation because you have a mediator who advocates for you before the judgment of God.

1 John 2:1-2

[2] My dear children, I write this to you so that you will not sin. But if anybody does sin, we have an advocate with the Father—Jesus Christ, the Righteous One. [2] He is the atoning sacrifice for our sins, and not only for ours but also for the sins of the whole world. (NIV)

Jesus' sacrifice is efficacious to pay for all the sins ever done by humanity. However, they are only appropriated by those who ask God for forgiveness of sin and redemption by Christ Jesus.

F. Key Recognition about World Religions:

As can be seen clearly there is a significant difference between Christianity and all other world religions. While most world religions hold that works count for eternity, or life after death. Only Christianity recognizes that your bad deeds can be covered by another. Every other religion assumes that somehow, some way, you either need to have more good deeds than bad, **or** that your ignorance will someday be dispelled, so that you can be enlightened enough to advance after death. Christianity has the works, the death and the resurrection of Christ Jesus. Jesus is your redeemer unto eternal life in those who accept God's offer of salvation through faith in His Son. It is never too late to make your request to Christ Jesus if you still live.

PART 9

How Can I be sure where I will spend Life after Death?

The various religions of the world have differing views on this idea. Some believe that if you do the works that they specify, that you need to accomplish in your lifetime, you will be destined to live in "heaven," "nirvana" or "paradise". These works have been mentioned in other sections of our Ten Big Question" such as Parts 6 and 8. I want to focus on what Christ and Christian writers have to say. Their guidelines or doctrine is substantially different from all the world religions.

A. **What is this Singularity?**

Christians believe and have been taught that it is not your works that bring you into heaven, but it is the works of Jesus Christ that allow you access to heaven. The reason that Jesus came into the world was to save the lost and to set the captives of Satan free. He does this by initiating a NEW Covenant between God and man.

B. The Two Covenants in the Scriptures:

As we saw earlier the first couple who God established on earth, were under a Covenant of Works. They had but ONE Commandment yet they would not even keep that commandment. Instead, they chose to rebel against God without fully realizing what the consequences would be. They took the fruit from the tree of Good and Evil and ate it. While they did not physically die immediately, this brought death to the earth and a curse upon all creation, that death would prevail throughout it. This disobedience or rebellion against God is defined as "sin" in the scriptures. Sin was a term used in archery meaning "to miss the mark." The idea of Original Sin is the moment when sin entered the world was when the first people did something that was contrary to the WILL and INSTRUCTION of God.

What is not evident when you read Genesis 3, is that Adam & Eve did die spiritually. This is the cause of their hiding from God, with whom previously they had a face-to-face relationship. They now knew EVIL, whereas before they only knew GOOD.

Genesis 3:8-13

> *8 Then the man and his wife heard the sound of the* Lord *God as he was walking in the garden in the cool of the day, and they hid from the* Lord *God among the trees of the garden. 9 But the* Lord *God called to the man, "Where are you?"*
>
> *10 He answered, "I heard you in the garden, and I was afraid because I was naked; so, I hid."*
>
> *11 And he said, "Who told you that you were naked? Have you eaten from the tree that I commanded you not to eat from?"*
>
> *12 The man said, "The woman you put here with me—she gave me some fruit from the tree, and I ate it."*

13 Then the LORD *God said to the woman, "What is this you have done?" The woman said, "The serpent deceived me, and I ate." (NIV)*

The fear of God is the evidence that they have changed significantly. However, there is another part of this story that further illustrates that Sin has cost the pair much. It is found in Genesis 3.

Genesis 3:21-24

21 The LORD *God made garments of skin for Adam and his wife and clothed them. 22 And the* LORD *God said, "The man has now become like one of us, knowing good and evil. He must not be allowed to reach out his hand and take also from the tree of life and eat, and live forever." 23 So the* LORD *God banished him from the Garden of Eden to work the ground from which he had been taken. 24 After he drove the man out, he placed on the east side of the Garden of Eden cherubim and a flaming sword flashing back and forth to guard the way to the tree of life. (NIV)*

The Disobedient pair had discovered they were naked before God and it frightened them, so they made a covering of leaves. God gives then a more permanent covering in the skins of animals. Now this may seem to you to be a nice thought, but so what. Let me confirm to you that nothing God ever does is insignificant. God gave them skins. In order that you and I have leather shoes or leather jackets, what must first happen…Yes, an animal had to die. This is the Holy God providing a sacrifice for the disobedient pair's sin, as a covering of their bodies but also as an atonement for their sin. This is where blood sacrifice enters into the world.

1 Peter 3:18

18 For Christ also suffered once for sins, the righteous for the unrighteous, to bring you to God. He was put to death in the body but made alive in the Spirit. (NIV)

What all people need to understand is that ten grams of sin is worse than 10,000 tons of good works. God was initiating a plan, that over time would come to the greatest sin offering the world has ever known. When the Son of Man, Jesus of Nazareth, goes to the cross, His death and spilled blood would pay for the collective SIN of all humanity.

C. <u>What must I do to inherit eternal Life:</u>

The desire of every person is to accomplish their salvation. This is in all religions of the world. Everyone, given our fallen state is looking to self-justify ourselves into heaven. We want to be able to obligate our judge into requiring our entry into heaven. We see a discussion that Jesus has with a young wealthy man, who was interested in assurance that he would have life after death. Matthew 19; Mark 10 and Luke 18 all record this discussion with the young man.

Matthew 19:16-21

> *[16] And behold, a man came up to him, saying, "Teacher, what good deed must I do to have eternal life?" [17] And he said to him, "Why do you ask me about what is good? There is only one who is good. If you would enter life, keep the commandments." [18] He said to him, "Which ones?" And Jesus said, "You shall not murder, You shall not commit adultery, You shall not steal, You shall not bear false witness, [19] Honor your father and mother, and, You shall love your neighbor as yourself." [20] The young man said to him, "All these I have kept. What do I still lack?" [21] Jesus said to him, "If you would be perfect, go, sell what you possess and give to the poor, and you will have treasure in heaven; and come, follow me." (ESV)*

We see here a man who thinks he qualifies but does not have assurance of his salvation. Jesus answers first with the law of God. But the young man says that he has lived a good life in keeping with the law. There is one thing that he is missing, that is "following Jesus". However, when Jesus suggests that it means giving up everything he has to follow Jesus the young man stumbles. Why does he stumble? Because he thinks that the things of this world are too great to give up for the next. Clearly he does not want Eternal life badly enough. The eternal question that Jesus asks everyone is "how much do you love me?" How much is the payment for your sin worth to you today?

D. <u>How do I access that Payment of Sin?</u>

The gift of eternal life is a free gift of God. It was provided by God through His Son Jesus, to bring us to God. It seems like an offer that is too simple, but when you look at the world religions as we have, the common finding of all is "what do I have to do to deserve heaven".

Mark 8:34-37

> *34 Then he called the crowd to him along with his disciples and said: "Whoever wants to be my disciple must deny themselves and take up their cross and follow me. 35 For whoever wants to save their life will lose it, but whoever loses their life for me and for the gospel will save it. 36 What good is it for someone to gain the whole world, yet forfeit their soul? 37 Or what can anyone give in exchange for their soul?. (NIV)*

This gift is accessed through the one thing that God counts as significant in His dominion, FAITH. If you trust that Jesus' payment is the perfect sacrifice, then you will be saved. This faith is a trust that goes to the efficacy of the sacrifice and to the truth of God in his provision for everyone.

If you do not trust God and His Son, then you will stand before a Holy and Just God with your works, when God, who scale of Justice is perfection, looks at your works. No one can expect to stand, given that God is not a God who judges on a curve, but upon His scale of Perfection and Truth.

E. **What will be the verdict for those who would offer God their works?**

When we recognize that there will be a final judgment for everyone, each of us need to be sure what is likely to be the outcome…

John 3:19-21

¹⁹ This is the verdict: Light has come into the world, but people loved darkness instead of light because their deeds were evil. ²⁰ Everyone who does evil hates the light and will not come into the light for fear that their deeds will be exposed. ²¹ But whoever lives by the truth comes into the light, so that it may be seen plainly that what they have done has been done in the sight of God. (NIV)

The truth that we need to live by is that we are absolutely bankrupt to stand before a Just and Holy God. If we claim, we did not know or we are not as bad as some these, we have empty pleas. Our only Hope is to be found trusting in the sacrifice of Jesus for us, then we are in a relationship with Him, going forward from today. Paul and Silas who were imprisoned in Philippi responded to their jailer who after an earthquake feared that all his prisoners had escaped and he would be held accountable with his life. When he realized that this was a sent to show him his vulnerability he asked Paul what He must do to be saved,

Acts 16:31.

³¹ They replied, "Believe in the Lord Jesus, and you will be saved—you and your household." (NIV)

The jailer was led to trust the truth of God's provision by the testimony of Paul and Silas from their prison cell. The jailer and his family were convinced that they could have a salvation purchased by Christ Jesus.

F. Assurance that I have eternal Life & forgiveness of Sins.

As John writes to the believers about eternal life and the forgiveness of sins, Jesus is now advocating with the Father for us who believe and are trusting in Jesus' righteousness and sacrifice. All we need to do is repent and to ask forgiveness. Jesus will intercede for you to forgive you of your sin, sins from before and sins after accepting Christ's provision.

1 John 2:1-2

> *²:¹ My dear children, I write this to you so that you will not sin. But if anybody does sin, we have an advocate with the Father—Jesus Christ, the Righteous One. ² He is the atoning sacrifice for our sins, and not only for ours but also for the sins of the whole world.* (NIV)

As Paul confirms in his letter to the church in Rome that the Christian must affirm the truth that Jesus is Lord of their lives and that by his bodily resurrection He proved His authority as the Son of God.

Romans 10:9-10

> *⁹ If you declare with your mouth, "Jesus is Lord," and believe in your heart that God raised him from the dead, you will be saved. ¹⁰ For it is with your heart that you believe and are justified, and it is with your mouth that you profess your faith and are saved. ¹¹ As Scripture says, "Anyone who believes in him will never be put to shame." ¹² For there is no difference between Jew and Gentile—the same Lord is Lord of all and richly blesses all who call on him, ¹³ for, "Everyone who calls on the name of the Lord will be saved."* (NIV)

There is a need to acknowledge the truth of Christ' sacrifice in your life. Anyone willing to accept the offer of forgiveness of sin will also trust the truth of who Jesus is and what He has done for them.

G. Why will God Forgive the sinner and pronounce Him Righteous to enter into Heaven?

Paul tells us in his letter to the Roman church that we have a righteousness imputed to us through Jesus our Saviour.

Romans 3:21- 26

²¹ But now apart from the law the righteousness of God has been made known, to which the Law and the Prophets testify. ²² This righteousness is given through faith in Jesus Christ to all who believe. There is no difference between Jew and Gentile, ²³ for all have sinned and fall short of the glory of God, ²⁴ and all are justified freely by his grace through the redemption that came by Christ Jesus. ²⁵ God presented Christ as a sacrifice of atonement, through the shedding of his blood—to be received by faith. He did this to demonstrate his righteousness, because in his forbearance he had left the sins committed beforehand unpunished—²⁶ he did it to demonstrate his righteousness at the present time, so as to be just and the one who justifies those who have faith in Jesus. (NIV)

H. Why will God Forgive the sinner and pronounce Him Righteous to enter into Heaven?

Can we be guaranteed to be reconciled to God, if we struggle with sin in our lives, even after we come to accept Christ as our Saviour? The answer according to Paul the Apostle is yes we can.

Romans 5:6-11

⁶ You see, at just the right time, when we were still powerless, Christ died for the ungodly. ⁷ Very rarely will anyone die for a righteous person, though for a good person someone might possibly dare to die. ⁸ But God demonstrates his own love for

us in this: While we were still sinners, Christ died for us. [9]
Since we have now been justified by his blood, how much
more shall we be saved from God's wrath through him! [10] For
if, while we were God's enemies, we were reconciled to him
through the death of his Son, how much more, having been
reconciled, shall we be saved through his life! [11] Not only is this
so, but we also boast in God through our Lord Jesus Christ,
through whom we have now received reconciliation. (NIV)

Jesus' sacrifice is efficacious to pay for all the sins ever done by humanity. However, they are only appropriated by those who ask God for forgiveness of sin and redemption by Christ Jesus. Jesus offers the world deliverance from the penalty of sin, but man always wants to bring his so-called good works into the final judgment because man want to be self-sustaining and not beholding to God.

I. Can I have assurance that my trust in Jesus is effective now and forever.

So, the Righteous and Just God of the Bible has lovingly offered up His own Son to be the redeemer, to pay for our law-breaking sins and rebellious inclinations. Once this payment was made, then to be considered righteous and justified to enter God's heaven and eternal life all that is necessary is to accept the gift of forgiveness and redemption of sins. By repenting of our sins and asking Jesus to cover over our sins with His righteousness, brings us into the family of God through the forgiveness of our sins by his sacrifice on the cross. Assurance of salvation and eternal life is that simple. It is not our works but His works that justify us.

John 14:1-8

[14:1] "Do not let your hearts be troubled. You believe in God;
believe also in me. [2] My Father's house has many rooms; if
that were not so, would I have told you that I am going there
to prepare a place for you? [3] And if I go and prepare a place
for you, I will come back and take you to be with me that

you also may be where I am. ⁴ You know the way to the place
where I am going." ⁵ Thomas said to him, "Lord, we don't
know where you are going, so how can we know the way?"
⁶ Jesus answered, "I am the way and the truth and the life.
No one comes to the Father except through me. ⁷ If you really
know me, you will know my Father as well. From now on,
you do know him and have seen him." ⁸ Philip said, "Lord,
show us the Father and that will be enough for us." (NIV)

As you can see by all of the above scriptures, the offer of forgiveness
of sins and the assurance of your destiny of heaven, is through the Saviour
Christ Jesus. All under heaven or on earth, will be judged the same way.
Are your sins forgiven and paid for permanently? Are you willing to accept
the offer that our perfect God has made for you?

When asked, the man on the street will say that he thinks God will
weigh his good deeds against his bad and judge man on a curve. A righteous
judge looks for proof of lawbreaking which is not hard to find in any man
or woman of this earth.

PART 10

Are Humans unique or just another Specie Among a cast of Thousands.

I Think therefore "I Am":

The Christians & Jews believe there is more to man than just Flesh & Bone:

This is founded upon the description we find in the scriptures, particularly the creation story of Adam & Eve. The intellect, self-awareness and conscience are expressed outside of the physical body. The existence of the conscience can be debated, but there is evidence that man has an in-built understanding of right and wrong, that is evident even in childhood. Ideas of right and wrong are somewhat cultural in nature, but there are cross-cultural barriers of right and wrong with surprising consistency. Theft, adultery, murder and parental authority are all examples of cross-cultural morals that stand up throughout all time and throughout all cultures. These are ideas that are not physical in nature, although they govern physical activities.

A. __Man is both Physical and Spiritual__

Therefore, the first idea of "What is Man," that we can recognize is, Man must be both physical and spiritual at the same time. Spiritual here, being a recognition that the thought process is outside of the physical realm, if it transcends the brain and the body. This nonphysical existence is something that differs from all other forms of life on earth. There is evidence that some animals can reason to some degree, but none can match humanity's powers of observation and reason. None can exhibit a conscience or operate according to laws governing their behavior, other than a rudimentary "act" and "react" processes. Furthermore, the concept of self-awareness is a concept of reasoning that is well beyond any other being in nature.

Monkeys can use tools to reach food, but none of them are likely going to write "Return to the Planet of the Apes". Crows are said to be able to recognize faces of friends or enemies, but none of them are authoring "War & Peace".

Remember that "information" is different from "data". Information is the recognizing of the significance of data. Data is the capturing and accumulation of factors either, by observation or quantification, in that "process portion" of understanding. The idea of understanding then, comes from recognition of the significance of factors that are accumulated. For example, when we sit down to read we have learned that certain symbols stand for specific sounds. When aggregated those sounds, they make up words the meaning of which we have learned over time. Finally, when see the whole in a greater context, such as this page, we can appraise the ideas with our own understand in a way that may lead to further subtlety of connections. This is evidence of reasoning & conceptualization sets humanity apart from all other species.

B. __Man has Volition, Rationality and Affection__

Humanity operates in a world of will or volition. We know what we want to do and can think of ways of doing it. However, we have in our volition, a sense of "ought" and "ought not". This is the extension and outward signs of consciousness.

Furthermore, when we consider what we want, there is a balancing act going on conceptually. This balancing or weighing act is how, we consider "the what", "the when", "the how" and "the why" of our wants. This is what we know as rational thought. Rational thought is a metaphysical concept. Metaphysical is being outside the physical. We may consider our "gut" feelings about something but this is not a sign of stomach problems. Nor is the desire of affections, a feeling somewhere in your underwear. Rational thought, feelings and desires of affection are metaphysical ideas that are not based in the physical material parts of man, but central to the spiritual part of man as is our conscience.

I am made of flesh & Bone therefore "I feel, see and measure!":

A. Atheist's concept of Man: We are only Material and therefore all is Brain function.

This atheist assumption is based upon the idea that we are only material (i.e., the brain and body). If it is not in the material body, then it must not exist, because it cannot be measured. This approach overlooks the fact that there are several things about us that are not material. Consider this. When we think of a concept such as "air", we can begin a process of measuring and determining what the components of air are. Air is a physical or material thing. However, to ask the question "what is air" can be measured by separating each of the components. But the question "why is there air" is not a physical thing, but a functional concept of imagining and conceptualizing. It is a brain function to some extent, but there is a higher plane here that conceives the idea. Ideas are not material; they transcend the physical limits of the brain. You may be able to measure some brain activity but that is not to say that it represents the full realm of conceptualizing or rational thought. They are notionally outside the realm of physical things.

Atheists believe that man is the sum of all his physical parts. They limit everything to only what can be measured in the makeup humanity. Therefore, the brain is the command center of the being. When the brain dies that is the end. Full Stop! There is no God, nor is there any life after

146

death. In order for there be life after death, there must be a judge who will determine good from evil. The judge will balance and judge our performance against the scale of good and evil.

As a result atheists postulate, there is no judge. There cannot be any determination of absolute good or evil. The atheist is the sole judge of himself and others around him. This leads naturally to the proposition that all things are relative in order. This assumes that political correctness is the determiner of right and wrong which is determined in relative determinations of each society. Each one will then make his own way in the world operating on his own value system responding to the trials and torments of the community, as it passes through various value judgments.

However anytime an individual makes a judgment about good and evil, he is determining it based upon the idea "that man is but a product of his own DNA and thoughts, which are functions of his material brain". Therefore, there really cannot be any guilt or innocence after all 'it is all a chemical reaction and brain function' that is the prime determiner of how we behave. Can chemistry really be judged? Like Adam and Eve, they lay the blame on someone or something outside themselves.

B. <u>Created by God Jewish concept of man:</u>

The Jewish idea of humanity comes from the writings of the Old Testament and the early writings of commentary and interpretation, found in the Mishnah. Basically, the Jewish idea of Man is that he is created physically with the body and spiritually in the soul. From Scripture, they see humanity has fallen from their beginning state. All humanity emanates from a First Pair, Adam & Eve. They were created by God as being "very good". They were created both with physical bodies with specific design to live and prosper upon the earth. They are also having a complete spiritual understanding of the goodness endowed in them and around them. "⁷ the LORD God formed the man from the dust of the ground and breathed into his nostrils the breath of life, and the man became a living being." (NIV) (Genesis 2:7). The soul being the spiritual part of the pair believed to be imparted when God breathed life into them.

However, in a tragic event, they choose to rebel against God. In that event, they caused themselves and the world around them to be cursed by God. In their fall from relationship with God into self-interest, they began what we now see in the world today:

➤ The existence of evil.
➤ The inevitability of death.
➤ A world that is filled with evidence of life and death.

The Jewish thought then, is that man is made up of two distinct parts – The body and the soul. The first being a measurable substance and the second being observable only in its activity of understanding, interpreting and conscience. In both, the Jewish and the Christian concept of man, the Soul is "eternal" but the body is temporal. Man is in fact then a "Soul with a body, while the body is subject to death and decay." In Jewish doctrine, the idea that there is a physical resurrection someday, is not mentioned in the first five books of the Torah. Therefore, some Jews are divided upon the subject to resurrection of the body. Whether souls in heaven or hell will possess bodies is an open question by different branches of Judaism. However, there is unanimous agreement as to the ultimate destinations – it is either heaven or hell.

In both, the Jewish and Christian view, humanity is fallen by sin and rebellion against God as recorded in the early scripture of the Bible. Because of his self-interest, he puts himself before all others, he is now under judgement of God. Furthermore, man's denial of his dependence on God's providence towards him, his lack of thankfulness to God his provider, all speak to the certainty of man's fallenness. (Romans 1:18-24) Man's religious bent speaks to His need and awareness that there is an accountability that man will face now and at some time in the future.

C. **The Christian Concept of Man:**

Similar to the Jewish concept of Man, the Christian understands that man is either – Body & Soul (a dichotomy) or as of Body, Soul and Spirit (a Trichotomy). As expressed above, the dichotomist considers man to have two parts from creation. The trichotomist understands that there was a spirit of God placed within man at creation that departed or died upon the fall of man. In Christianity, the essence of what Man is; that he has a physical part that is subject to death and decay. He also has a soul or soul and Spirit which is eternal and subject to the outcomes of eternity. Man is also destined to go after death to either Heaven, an existence in the presence of God or Hell in an existence without God. In Genesis 1:26-28 Moses gives us a description of the origin of humanity.

> *26 Then God said, "Let us make man in our image, after our likeness. And let them have dominion over the fish of the sea and over the birds of the heavens and over the livestock and over all the earth and over every creeping thing that creeps on the earth."*
>
> *27 So God created man in his own image, in the image of God he created him; male and female he created them.*
>
> *28 And God blessed them. And God said to them, "Be fruitful and multiply and fill the earth and subdue it, and have dominion over the fish of the sea and over the birds of the heavens and over every living thing that moves on the earth."*
> *(ESV)*

Theologians have discussed this for thousands of years as to what God meant by making man in His own image. The short answer for our purposes is that we are made with a soul/spirit and a body. Like God, we can conceptualize ideas and thoughts. Like God, we can communicate those thoughts and ideas to one another in language. The letters of language that is written is data…language that is spoken or read is information because it contains ideas and conceptualizations. You can see this specifically as you read this book. The printed letters (data) make up words that over time you have learned as concepts by how they are used and specifically here now as they are used. The ideas and thoughts you have are evident of your ability to process data and which are evidence of a human soul.

Man being made up of body and Spirit/Soul means that we are both material and immaterial at the same time. It is this dualism that differentiates us for all others in creation. It is through this dualism that God made man to be compatible with God. In Genesis 3:8, we see that the first pair were regularly in relationship with God. However, after they had fallen into sin they were afraid of the presence of God. Somehow they were aware that the compatibility of man with God had been broken by their disobedience to the one command God had given them.

The Fall of Man:

Both Christians & Jews hold to the idea that creation started out "good" with man experiencing a loving communion with God. However, being volitional humanity had but one command in the garden.

Genesis 2:15-17

> *¹⁵ The* Lord *God took the man and put him in the Garden of Eden to work it and take care of it. ¹⁶ And the* Lord *God commanded the man, "You are free to eat from any tree in the garden; ¹⁷ but you must not eat from the tree of the knowledge of good and evil, for when you eat of it you will surely die."* (NIV)

We do not know what this tree was; the important idea here was the Prohibition of God rather than was it poisonous or otherwise harm filled.

Unfortunately, mankind's progenitors, Adam & Eve chose to break God's one and only command. Then death came into the world through the curse of man for his disobedience. This punishment is reflective of two especially important concepts, the Sovereignty of God and the Holiness of God. God is not a being like us, who can be transgressed against without His imposing punishment. His laws radiate from His character and there is no marking on the curve with Him. His grace and mercy must be consistent with His righteousness and justice. When we transgress His commands, there is a requirement that every sin must be paid for in time;

(from murder to fits of rage, from perjury to white lies or from adultery to impure thoughts).

While the first pair lived according to God's one command, there was eternal life and goodness in all things. When the pair, the pinnacle of creation, sinned, they sinned against God. Then death was the penalty imposed upon the earth. It was imposed because God's covenant with Adam and Eve was do not eat…or you will surely die. The first humans chose to break that covenant which brought judgment and death upon humanity and the earth.

In Psalm 8, there is a poetical account of man's fortunate place in creation.

Psalm 8:1-9

¹Lord, our Lord, how majestic is your name in all the earth! You have set your glory in the heavens. ² Through the praise of children and infants you have established a stronghold against your enemies, to silence the foe and the avenger. ³ When I consider your heavens, the work of your fingers, the moon and the stars, which you have set in place, ⁴ what is mankind that you are mindful of them, human beings that you care for them? ⁵ You have made them a little lower than the angels and crowned them with glory and honor. ⁶ You made them rulers over the works of your hands; you put everything under their feet: ⁷ all flocks and herds, and the animals of the wild, ⁸ the birds in the sky, and the fish in the sea, all that swim the paths of the seas. ⁹ Lord, our Lord, how majestic is your name in all the earth!(NIV)

Humanity has been given a privileged place in creation from the start. However, humanity has lost the status they held first had when created. Being fully compatible with God, they are now in need of an intermediary to restore their compatibility with God. On earth today, our compatibility with God can be restored, through the Intercession of Jesus Christ, who has paid the debt that humanity incurred when they fell from the grace of God, through their disobedient lawlessness.

Those who would argue that a loving God would not subject man to an eternity in torment with the absence of God, do not recognize that God is perfect in all His ways. His Love and His justice are both perfect. In His teaching on this subject, Jesus points out that man has three things with which his final destination is impacted.

> ➢ The creation surrounding him which speaks of the existence of God.
> ➢ Man's conscience which speaks to the basis of right and wrong, is imprinted in his mind.
> ➢ The record of God speaking to man:
>   o The Biblical record.
>   o The sending of Jesus His Son into the world to teach about the Kingdom of God and to die as an atonement for man's sin.

With these, humanity has a way out of a destiny of eternity without God, in hell. Man can choose to follow the narrow path in Christ Jesus to heaven. (Matthew 7:13-14; Matthew 7:21-23; Luke 13:23-25; Luke 13:26-2; Luke 6:46; John 14:23-24; Mark 4:15-17; James 4:4; Isaiah 35:8 and 1 John 3:8-10).

Man has a lifetime on earth to choose whether to depend on what Jesus Christ has done for him or to reject the offer of eternal life in Christ Jesus. This decision to accept and trust in Jesus' payment is a decision to trust God's own provision, which brings you to a life in heaven with God for eternity. A rejection will mean that you have rejected God himself. You are destined yourself to live an eternity without the presence of God and Christ Jesus.

There is no other method by which man can avoid his destiny. No works of man can make up for the selfish interest and deeds that humanity has done upon earth in this life. All these deeds and thoughts are known by an Omniscient God, who will judge us by our own deeds and thoughts. Only those who know and trust Jesus for their salvation, will be judged righteous by God at the final judgement that comes, either at our death or upon the final return of Christ Jesus to earth.

What does the bible teach about the soul?

In both the Old Testament and new testament there are more than 700 of mentions in scripture for the in Greek & Hebrew that are translated as "Soul" and "Spirit" each. In each of these is found the teaching of the existence of a soul/spirit. The teaching is that the soul and spirit is unseen, immaterial and spiritual realm. The body belongs to the visible physical material world. When we take the Old and New Testaments we find a consistent metanarrative about how humanity has been affected by their rebellion and how God is making provision to redeem him. It is essential that man's soul plays out as a key factor through redemptive history. There is a significant difference to the idea of a soul in man, being significantly different from the animal world. In the new testament the soul is destined to being either in heaven with God or in danger in torment in hell where God is not present.

In a parable about two different men who die and each is sent to separate destinies.

Luke 16:19-31 The Rich Man and Lazarus

19 "There was a rich man who was clothed in purple and fine linen and who feasted sumptuously every day. 20 And at his gate was laid a poor man named Lazarus, covered with sores, 21 who desired to be fed with what fell from the rich man's table. Moreover, even the dogs came and licked his sores. 22 The poor man died and was carried by the angels to Abraham's side. The rich man also died and was buried, 23 and in Hades, being in torment, he lifted up his eyes and saw Abraham far off and Lazarus at his side. 24 And he called out, 'Father Abraham, have mercy on me, and send Lazarus to dip the end of his finger in water and cool my tongue, for I am in anguish in this flame.' 25 But Abraham said, 'Child, remember that you in your lifetime received your good

things, and Lazarus in like manner bad things; but now he is comforted here, and you are in anguish. ²⁶ And besides all this, between us and you a great chasm has been fixed, in order that those who would pass from here to you may not be able, and none may cross from there to us.' ²⁷ And he said, 'Then I beg you, father, to send him to my father's house—²⁸ for I have five brothers—so that he may warn them, lest they also come into this place of torment.' ²⁹ But Abraham said, 'They have Moses and the Prophets; let them hear them.' ³⁰ And he said, 'No, father Abraham, but if someone goes to them from the dead, they will repent.' ³¹ He said to him, 'If they do not hear Moses and the Prophets, neither will they be convinced if someone should rise from the dead.'" (ESV)*

From this parable of Jesus, we can see that each man has been judged by God and directed after death to significantly different destines. In this parable there is fixed between the two destinies a great impassable gulf. This gulf is fixed into eternity and is impassible either within the realm of their destiny nor back into this world. The basis of the judgment is really not plumbed, so we will take it as revealed that further information is needed in this. There is a judgment of each Human which will determine their destiny after death. Furthermore, there appears from some of the teachings of Jesus and Paul, that we will be known and recognize others when we reach our destiny after death.

However, there are several aspect of the soul that we can discern in the Christian concept of the soul. The judgment of the human will determine the permeant destination of the soul.

Matthew 10:28

"And do not fear those who kill the body but are unable to kill the soul; but rather fear Him who is able to destroy both ***soul*** *and body in hell."* (NIV)

Matthew 16:26

²⁶ What good will it be for someone to gain the whole world, yet forfeit their soul? Or what can anyone give in exchange for their soul? (NIV)

There is also evidence that in the teachings of Jesus and Paul the apostle that the destiny of some souls is the be with Christ after death. We see this in several specific places in scripture. *(Luke 23:39-43, 2 Corinthians 5:1-8).* In fact, on the night He would be betrayed, Jesus promise that He is going to prepare a place for His disciples and He will return to bring them to that place.

John 14:1-4 Jesus Comforts His Disciples

¹⁴:¹ "Do not let your hearts be troubled. You believe in God; believe also in me. ² My Father's house has many rooms; if that were not so, would I have told you that I am going there to prepare a place for you? ³ And if I go and prepare a place for you, I will come back and take you to be with me that you also may be where I am. ⁴ You know the way to the place where I am going."(NIV)

The soul is the God given source that animates the body. When death comes that soul leaves and then death occurs. In his teachings, Solomon the author of Proverbs and Ecclesiastes defines the moment of death in the verses below.

Ecclesiastes 12:6-7

Remember him—before the silver cord is severed, and the golden bowl is broken; before the pitcher is shattered at the spring, and the wheel broken at the well, ⁷ and the dust returns to the ground it came from, and the spirit returns to God who gave it. *(NIV)*

In His teaching on the life being in the soul, Jesus when asked a question about the resurrection, has a very powerful response to His questioner.

Matthew 22:23-33 Marriage at the Resurrection

23 That same day the Sadducees, who say there is no resurrection, came to him with a question. 24 "Teacher," they said, "Moses told us that if a man dies without having children, his brother must marry the widow and raise up offspring for him. 25 Now there were seven brothers among us. The first one married and died, and since he had no children, he left his wife to his brother. 26 The same thing happened to the second and third brother, right on down to the seventh. 27 Finally, the woman died. 28 Now then, at the resurrection, whose wife will she be of the seven, since all of them were married to her?"

29 Jesus replied, "You are in error because you do not know the Scriptures or the power of God. 30 At the resurrection people will neither marry nor be given in marriage; they will be like the angels in heaven. 31 But about the resurrection of the dead—have you not read what God said to you, 32 'I am the God of Abraham, the God of Isaac, and the God of Jacob'? He is not the God of the dead but of the living." 33 When the crowds heard this, they were astonished at his teaching. (NIV)

What Jesus has clarified for the questioners is more than there are no marriages in heaven; BUT that Abraham, Isaac and Jacob are alive today and living in conscious awareness with God in heaven. So, without doubt the teachings of Jesus convey certainty that there is life after death. Such a life is in the soul who is immortal.

In the Spiritual realm, there is awareness of other souls. There is an inner awareness of the soul that seek a permanent restoration to that which was God's first design. This permanent restoration is spoken of as a resurrection of the body and a restoration of the soul and body in a transformed identity which will be in a new immortal body, soul and spirit entity of God's recreation.

2 Corinthians 3:1-8 Awaiting the New Body

5:1 For we know that if the earthly tent we live in is destroyed, we have a building from God, an eternal house in heaven, not built by human hands. ² Meanwhile we groan, longing to be clothed instead with our heavenly dwelling, ³ because when we are clothed, we will not be found naked. ⁴ For while we are in this tent, we groan and are burdened, because we do not wish to be unclothed but to be clothed instead with our heavenly dwelling, so that what is mortal may be swallowed up by life. ⁵ Now the one who has fashioned us for this very purpose is God, who has given us the Spirit as a deposit, guaranteeing what is to come. ⁶ Therefore we are always confident and know that as long as we are at home in the body we are away from the Lord. ⁷ For we live by faith, not by sight. ⁸ We are confident, I say, and would prefer to be away from the body and at home with the Lord. (NIV)

We understand that at creation God imparted into man the soul that represents all that man would be and would become. This endowed a dignity to every person on earth through all history. Being image bearers in the Soul of man, there is no person without dignity nor with less dignity regardless of their capabilities, colour, class or age. All persons from preborn or newborn, bedridden or on their death bed have equal value to God. In all Christian communities, the value of all humanity is given equal dignity because of the immortal soul they possess.

When we consider the evidence that there is in humanity, we know there is a significant difference between what constitutes man and what constitutes all other beings or species on earth. There is ample weight to know that humanity is substantially different from all other species. Man's self-awareness and his ability to formulate complicated concepts and communicate these accurately to one another so that full understanding is both complete and can be transferred onto others.

Man, and Mother Nature:

In today's western society, there is a blurring of the condition of man as being distinct from nature. Many believe that we humans are just another specie in the mix of many species. Therefore, we have no right of dominance or connection, to the natural beings that surround us in nature. This leads to the belief, that man is the problem for nature, and that man is not part of nature. Therefore, some advocate for species over man because of man's negative influence in nature.

However, in evolutionary philosophy, man has evolved from previous life forms, through gene mutation that leads to where we are today. This brings with it a premise, "that all forms that progress are done so because they are better at adapting to the environment". No one thinks about the consequences, which come from such an assumption. The consequences are, that those species that fail to adapt go extinct because they are no longer effective. Therefore, to blame humanity for these extinctions is contrary to the basic premises of evolution.

Christian view of man and nature:

While humanity does have an effect on other species, there is a certainty that man is prime in the order of all things in nature. Therefore, humanity has both a responsibility to protect nature and to understand nature. It is a mistake to blur the line as to man's accountability to nature and lower beings. Humanity's first priority is to the community of man in the order even though humanity has accountability to protect nature.

"Historic Christianity sees man as distinct, but not divorced, from nature. On the level of his personhood, man is distinct from the rest of finite creation. He is to find complete fulfillment for his aspirations only in God. But on the level of his finiteness, man is one within nature as part of the wider finite creation. Thus, despite real differences, man has relationship to nature that is the source of his responsibility and his respect for it."[5]

Therefore, we need to be careful when considering all of nature in relation to man. There is no avoiding the issue that man is the protector of nature but man is not subservient to the natural order. There is a great error in thinking that beasts of creation are to be given preference to humanity.

The Historical Account of Redemptive Transformation of Mankind.

In classic Christianity, man undergoes transformation in development over time. The stages of redemptive history can be listed as follows:

The Innocence – From creation of Man he was without sin knowing only very good as God declares in Genesis 1:31. Adam and Eve knew no evil and lived according to God's authority to fill the earth and have dominion over all creation. Adam was in full communion with God in his daily life., Adam and Eve exercised authority over creation. This authority was a delegated directly from God. It was based upon the relationship with God in His Goodness. Adam and Eve in this state were fully compatible with God.

The Naturalist – In the Garden, Adam was given work in the garden of Eden. He was to expand the garden to fill the whole earth. He was to name the animals and discover all that was in the garden. His one prohibition was that Adam and Eve were not to eat the fruit of only one tree in the garden -the tree of knowledge of good & evil. God had warned them that, if they did breach that prohibition that, they would die. When the couple, who were the only two humans in existence, choose to rebel against God then death did come into the earth. Nature and man alike were subject to death.

There are three aspects of the curse of death that we need to understand. First, is that as they were the first humans their sin and rebellion was accounted to every new human who came to be born after them. Adam

---

[5] Guinness, Os. (1973). The Dust of Death. InterVarsity Press (p. 207). Downers Grove, Illinois: 60515.

knew what he was doing when he sinned. He became the carrier of this sinful nature. Eve who was deceived became the barer of the line of fallen humanity. Therefore, the second devastating effect of sin is that death was transferred into the nature of every human born to woman. Man's image was now distorted with selfishness, guilt and shame. (Genesis 3:10) Their fellowship with God was now severed and they were without hope. The third effect of sin was that into nature, death and distortion came upon nature. Since then nature has been infected with a curse (Genesis 3:17-18). The curse also affected nature in as it manifests "red in blood and claw." Evolutionist would attribute this to "survival of the fittest"; Christianity attribute this to the fall of man infecting all of nature which along with man will someday be redeemed.

The Graciously Saved – With the beginning of the New Testament era, we see the coming of the promised Messiah, who brought hope, forgiveness and grace to humanity. Jesus began His mission to the world, by explaining the laws of God based upon the Old Testament scriptures. He revealed a new and overwhelming hope, that humanity may once again have a fellowship with the Living God. Humanity needed a Saviour, who would provide a payment for man's sins. Jesus would fully redeem man from His grievous sin debt against God. However, let us recognize that to receive this salvation man must admit he is in rebellion to God and ask for forgiveness. In this repentance he will receive the promised salvation. As they are now saved, they need to be declared righteous before God who graciously restored each man who asked for that salvation. The righteousness that Christ brings, having lived a sinless life, is now imputed to every sinner who repents of his sin and asks to be forgiven. Having been forgiven those, who are in Christ receive the Holy Spirit as a seal for their redemption unto eternal life.

2 Corinthians 1:21-23

21 Now it is God who makes both us and you stand firm in Christ. He anointed us, 22 set his seal of ownership on us, and put his Spirit in our hearts as a deposit, guaranteeing what is to come. 23 I call God as my witness—and I stake my life on it—that it was in order to spare you that I did not return to Corinth. *(NIV)*

Glorified – Those who are the redeemed of Christ, are now adopted into the family of God. Those alive in this condition are living a life under the promise of eternal life with God, and while on earth experience the fellowship with God and in empowerment of the Holy Spirit, to live a life of growing holiness and sanctification. The ultimate arrival into glory is based, upon the actual resurrection of Christ from the grave. His resurrection is the guarantee that the children of God will be resurrected, either on earth at the second coming of Christ or in heaven, which is our destiny should we die before Christs second advent (coming).

Along with humanity being redeemed so to will all of nature, the prophet Isaiah foresaw it even before Christ came to earth,

Isaiah 11:6-9

⁶ The wolf will live with the lamb, the leopard will lie down with the goat, the calf and the lion and the yearling together; and a little child will lead them. ⁷ The cow will feed with the bear, their young will lie down together, and the lion will eat straw like the ox.

⁸ The infant will play near the cobra's den, and the young child will put its hand into the viper's nest. ⁹ They will neither harm nor destroy on all my holy mountain, for the earth will be filled with the knowledge of the Lord *as the waters cover the sea.* *(NIV)*

CONCLUSION

When I look at the various ideas about what is man, I am impressed with several conclusions. The first, that is the diversity in the understandings of man among religions. There is a large variance that can be rationalize among the world views they hold. Each one assumes and professes to have the ultimate answer to truth about the origin and understanding of man.

The second idea is that man is clearly and significantly different from all other species upon the earth. Man exhibits spiritual or metaphysical characteristics that separate him from the rest of creation. As such, his significance must be caused by some difference in makeup that would signal to all observers that he is not just any ordinary being like all the others. Many animals can communicate to one another, but there is a substantial difference between the writers of the American Constitution and what passes for whale communications.

There are several common ideas in terms of general statements, but there are significant variances. First the idea of who man is; most, except for atheists, agree that man is spiritual and physical,. There are statements about heaven & hell that are similar, however, some assume you need to work your way into heaven. The exception is Christianity, who say that it is by the finished work of Christ that you gain heaven. There is the issue of evil and suffering which some say, are an illusion or misunderstanding, while Christianity & Judaism say it came through the fall of humanity in our progenitors, Adam & Eve.

So, as we consider man and the other questions, we cannot conclude that all religions are the same. By logical extension, if one of them is true, then the others must be false. All religions make truth claims that are exclusive. No one religion is fully compatible with all others... So where are we in looking at the ten most important questions? I think that we have arrived at the crossroad of serious decision.

Some Further Considerations:

The concept of the Christians Triune God is a very big philosophical idea. It is not well understood by many people but it is the foundation of everything Christian. In fact, if you reject the Trinity, you cannot call yourself a Christian. If you see the trinity as various modes by which God reveals Himself, then you have missed to idea of the personality of God and fallen it the heresy of Modalism.

Why is this important?

This is important, because if your comprehension of God is always going to be slightly off. God is eternal all-knowing, and we are temporal knowing in part. You can only know and understand God, by the ways he has revealed Himself to us. Our future in Christ Jesus is going to be, learning more and more about our God. However, today we need to look only one place, to be able to see and comprehend God.

John 1:1-14

1:1 In the beginning was the Word, and the Word was with God, and the Word was God. 2 He was with God in the beginning. 3 Through him all things were made; without him nothing was made that has been made. 4 In him was life, and that life was the light of all mankind. 5 The light shines in the darkness, and the darkness has not overcome it. 6 There was a man sent from God whose name was John. 7 He came as a witness to testify concerning that light, so that through him all might believe. 8 He himself was not the light; he came only as a witness to the light.

⁹ The true light that gives light to everyone was coming into the world. ¹⁰ He was in the world, and though the world was made through him, the world did not recognize him. ¹¹ He came to that which was his own, but his own did not receive him. ¹² Yet to all who did receive him, to those who believed in his name, he gave the right to become children of God—¹³ children born not of natural descent, nor of human decision or a husband's will, but born of God. ¹⁴ The Word became flesh and made his dwelling among us. We have seen his glory, the glory of the one and only Son, who came from the Father, full of grace and truth. (NIV)

As we see, early on in the Old Testament, man wanted to see God face to face, and to be able to understand and to comprehend Him. However, the warning given to Moses and many others was, that you could not look upon the face of God and live. So, God Chose to send His Son, FULLY God and FULLY man, into the World, so that they could begin to understand God better. They would never fully understand God because God's fullness is complete in Himself. God chose to incarnate as a living human, who was to be born of a woman, so that humanity would be able to understand; what God is really like. From the scriptures, we are told that this was Jesus of Nazareth. A being like us, born human into the world; but unlike us was fully man and fully God. This was a radical idea, which was rejected by the men of his time and throughout history, because they saw Jesus and thought he was only a man. It was obvious, that this man was not ordinary, because as Nicodemus a Pharisee who came to Jesus, testified that *"Rabbi (teacher), we know that you are a teacher who has come from God, for no one could perform the signs you are doing if God were not with him." (John 3:2)*

Furthermore, when Jesus is preparing to go to the cross, He is having the "last" Passover Supper with his disciples and He has a conversation that has far reaching implications to this humanity & divinity of Jesus.

John 14:1-14 I Am the Way, and
the Truth, and the Life

14 _"Let not your hearts be troubled. Believe in God; believe also in me._ ² _In my Father's house are many rooms. If it were not so, would I have told you that I go to prepare a place for you?_ ³ _And if I go and prepare a place for you, I will come again and will take you to myself, that where I am you may be also._ ⁴ _And you know the way to where I am going."_ ⁵ _Thomas said to him, "Lord, we do not know where you are going. How can we know the way?"_ ⁶ _Jesus said to him, "I am the way, and the truth, and the life. No one comes to the Father except through me._ ⁷ _If you had known me, you would have known my Father also. From now on you do know him and have seen him."_

⁸ _Philip said to him, "Lord, show us the Father, and it is enough for us."_ ⁹ _Jesus said to him, "Have I been with you so long, and you still do not know me, Philip? Whoever has seen me has seen the Father. How can you say, 'Show us the Father'?_ ¹⁰ _Do you not believe that I am in the Father and the Father is in me? The words that I say to you I do not speak on my own authority, but the Father who dwells in me does his works._ ¹¹ _Believe me that I am in the Father and the Father is in me, or else believe on account of the works themselves._

¹² _"Truly, truly, I say to you, whoever believes in me will also do the works that I do; and greater works than these will he do, because I am going to the Father._ ¹³ _Whatever you ask in my name, this I will do, that the Father may be glorified in the Son._ ¹⁴ _If you ask me anything in my name, I will do it._ (ESV)

He tells them that, if you have seen me, you have seen the Father. Then He goes on to an exclusive statement. "I am the way the Truth and the Life. No one comes to the Father except through Me." This leaves no doubt that Jesus is laying claim to being the one and only way to God. Finally, He make a statement that is even more astounding.

"I am in the Father and the Father is in me". This unity is what underlines the concept of the Trinity.

R.C. Sproul spoke about this from the transcript from "Your Christ is too Small":

> "Jesus is the Word of God. He is the Wisdom of God, the Incarnate Wisdom of God. He is the perfect expression of God. God knows we want to see Him, but we can't, so He says: "If you want to see Me, look at Jesus. You want to know me? Look at Jesus. *'This is My beloved Son, Hear Him' (Matt. 17:5)*. My words are in His mouth.

> Jesus is called the Word of God(John 1:1-2) because He brings the Word of God, and He brings the Word of God because He is the Word of God. Jesus is called the truth because He speaks the truth, and He speaks the truth because He is the truth."[6]

This the best assessment of my thinking and my faith that I have ever read aside from the sixty-six books of the Bible. I leave you to meditate upon these words.

---

[6] Special transcript from a six-part teaching series by R.C. Sproul titled "Your Christ is Too Small."

Doorway, Granada, Spain

ADDENDUM 1: ISLAM

Q1. Does God exist?

❖ Islam believes in a Spiritual God who is all powerful. He is sovereign over all of the earth and no one can escape authority or sovereignty. God is great is the fundamental idea of Islam. It is represented in the Islamic "Allahu Akbar" which is translated as 'God is Great or literally 'God is greater". This is what you hear from the muezzin's voice in the call to prayer in every mosque. Many Mosques may allow Arabic writing on the outside of a mosque "Allahu Akbar". There is great reverence in this saying and it is the fundamental foundation of Islam. The oneness or unity of Allah is a fundamental all through the various versions of Islam (Sura 112.)

❖ That Muhammad is God's messenger (prophet) is also foundational to Islam. The Qur'an is the message that Muhammad recorded from God. Treatment of God's messenger is also held to a very high standard. Any criticism of him or his message is considered blasphemous.

❖ The fundamental idea of the nature of God is that He is a personal God but there is no possibility of humans interacting directly with Him. His will is to be obeyed and followed.

❖ Islam has a great aversion to the idea of idolatry(sura 112) and hence they allow no images of Allah or Muhammad.

❖ Islam contends that God exists without doubt and He is to be worshipped with care and wholehearted devotion

Q2. What has God Said?

❖ According to Islam God has spoken through His messenger Muhammad and that is represented in the Arabic record of Muhammad in the Qur'an. In his early writings, Muhammad endorse the Biblical writers (Moses & the prophets) as well as the prophetic office of Jesus. (Sura 3:3; 5:43-44, 47 & 58).

❖ However, in subsequent commentaries on the Qur'an, known as the Hadith, there is a position that Muhammad was talking about the original writers, but says that there have been many errors by the copyists that the Christian & Jewish Bible is no longer reliable.

❖ What Muhammad recorded in the Qur'an also gives more weight to the later writings, than the early revelation of the Qur'an. So, when there appears to be a conflict in Muhammad's writing, you would favour the later revelations over the earlier one. The Hadith writers establishing this precept on their own.

Q3. What is God like?

❖ For Islam God is sovereign and to be obeyed as in the relationship of master//slave. It is expected to obey rather than understand.

❖ Prayer is seen as a fundamental of worship and the prayers are generally formatted for everyone to follow together.

❖ God is self-sufficient and in all ways without need of anything.

❖ God is beyond our understanding and the human heart and mind cannot even grasp his greatness.

Q4. Who is Jesus of Nazareth?

❖ Jesus is seen by Islam as a great teacher and prophet.

❖ If they can be assured that a Muslim can know accurately what Jesus taught then and only then, should his teaching be considered.

❖ There is consensus that Jesus was born to a virgin. However, there is great doubt as to the crucifixion, then resurrection of Jesus. Hence Islam will not allow Jesus to be the Son of God, because it is blasphemous to add anything to the self-sufficiency of Allah.

Q5. What does Jesus offer us Today?

❖ Islam is not prepared to study Jesus because His word is suspect over time according to the writers of the Hadith regardless of what Mohammad wrote.

Q6. What happens when you Die?

❖ **Islam's idea of After life?**

❖ The Qur'an teaches that the human is a body/soul duality in existence. When the physical body dies, the soul is separated and is transferred into the afterlife. Death is determined and known by God, Allah. The timing is set at conception, but your destiny is determined by your worldly life - in deeds and words. One will be destined for the afterlife. The separation of the soul from the body is understood to be a painful event. There is an expectation that the body needs to be buried quickly in order to facilitate this separation permanently.

❖ According to a Hadith (commentary, Sahih al Bukharith) the "prophet Muhammad" dipped his hands in water and wiped his face saying, "there is no god but Allah; indeed, death has its pangs," then died. The idea of what heaven is like is different, based on different interpretations of the Qur'an. There is an idea that there is an afterlife bodily resurrection which is a different body than the one buried.

❖ In death, the buried person will be evaluated by two angels, "Munkar & Nakir", who will test the dead soul's understanding and faith. Those judged acceptable, progress into heaven in the resurrection body. Those who do not, are sent to Sijjin, which is a place of eternal punishment.

❖ The righteous believer is taken into the mercy and pleasure of God. However, there is a period of "Barzakh", in which the believer awaits the resurrection, because they have not achieved resurrection, until God fixes it so. For the believer, after judgement, they will go either to Jannah (heaven) or to Jahannam (Hell).

"Barzakh" is much like the idea of "limbo" as you wait for the final resurrection.

Q7. Why is there Evil in the World?

❖ Islam teaches that man has an inner conscience that directs him to know good from evil (fitrah). This sense is implanted in man from birth.

❖ While man is able to choose, Allah can intercede in a man's decision-making at will. Allah will never do evil but we are not able to understand the reasons for Allah doing anything.

❖ Islam believes that the source of Evil is selfishness in man. People can overcome this evil of selfishness, by easing the suffering of others. Others are generally assumed to be other Muslims.

Q8. Are All Religions the same Idea?

❖ Islam believes that all other religions are deceived and unless you convert to Islam you are destined to hell.

❖ Islam believes that if you will not convert then you should either be enslaved or put to death. The idea of Jihad is the carrying out a holy war against all other religions based upon the premise that as you are destined to hell then if you will not convert, then anytime is right to send you there.

Q9. How Can I be sure where I will spend Life after Death?

❖ Islam believes that God is transcendent from humanity. Allah is viewed as the creator of the universe and the source of all goodness. Everything happens as Allah's wills. Allah is powerful; a strict judge, who is also merciful towards His followers. Depending upon their life's good works and the Five-way path of Islam, which specifies those good works, determine where you will spend eternity:
  • Repeat the creed about Allah and Mohammad as your statement of faith.

- Recite certain prayers in Arabic five times daily.
- Give to the needy.
- One month each year fast from food, drink, sex and smoking from sunrise to sunset.
- Take a pilgrimage once in your life to worship at a shrine in Mecca.

Based upon these five duties, a Muslim hopes to enter paradise. If he dies a martyr's death then there is a promise of immediate entrance into paradise.

Q10. Are Humans unique or just another Species?

- ❖ The concept of man then, is as the obedient servant of Allah, following Mohammad's course of obligations, as recorded in the Qur'an and the writings of the early fathers of the faith, captured in the Hadith. The essence of Islam is that man is altogether other than Allah. They are in effect rejecting the idea that when God made man there is no likeness of Allah in man.
- ❖ If you ask a Muslim what Allah thinks of humanity, he will tell you that the Qur'an is filled with instruction for all levels of man from savage to sophisticated(learned). The essence of the teachings of the Qur'an and the worship of Allah is to bring man up to a spiritual being of wisdom and understanding.
- ❖ There is no difference in many branches of Islam, with the main branches being Sunni & Shi'a. Others are Ahmadiyya & Ibadi. Each has division being based around the one entitled to ascend to the leadership after Mohammod's death.

Garden pathway, Granada, Spain

ADDENDUM 2: EASTERN RELIGIONS

Hinduism

Q1. Does God exist?

- ❖ The over-arching idea of Hinduism is that the problem of man is his separation from God. Largely God is an ultimate conglomeration of the eternal spirit unto which all living things belong.
- ❖ We have become divorced from reality of the one true Spirit; that all life is a search to reconnect to this Spiritual monism that unites every living thing.
- ❖ Pantheism is the belief that reality is identical with divinity, or that all-things compose an all-encompassing, transcendent god. All is God and all things end up in the same ultimate reality.
- ❖ Hindus recognize individual gods who figure is the early writing of Hinduism. In the polytheism version of Hinduism many Gods are recognized as pathways to the ultimate Brahman.

Q2. What has God Said?

- ❖ There is a great diversity of authority on who speaks "truth" in Hinduism. The term often given for authority is "guru". They can be anyone who is recognized as an authority and has an audience.
- ❖ There are several Hindu holy books that are recognized as authority. They are found in the tradition of the Veda's ("Knowledge"),

which are authored by several different members of the Brahman caste.

❖ These are recognized as authoritative, in a way that is documented in the earliest Hindu writings, which are divided into four volumes dating roughly to 1500BC.
- the Rig-Veda, a book of Mantras
- the Sama Veda, a book of songs
- the Yajur Veda, a book of rituals
- the Atharva Veda, a book of spells & charms

❖ There is no real consensus to the use or of these other than to press one into meditation that will lead you into oneness with the spirit and into denial of the individual.

Q3. What is God like?

❖ Hinduism springs from a pantheistic idea of the supernatural and a cyclical idea of time.

❖ Hinduism is both Pantheistic and polytheistic.

❖ Polytheism assumes that many gods exist and each needs to be placated in some way, to ensure that life today and life in the afterlife will be improved.

❖ The concept of God is that all is god and the main purpose of man is meditation unto oneness.

Q4. Who is Jesus of Nazareth?

❖ Jesus would not rate great significance to Hindus because his ideas of monotheism would run counter to Hinduism.

Q5. What does Jesus offer us Today?

❖ Jesus is not recognized as the son of God although some of his teachings would be valued by Hindus.

Q6. What happens when you Die?

❖ The process of rebirth is cyclic in nature. The process is called samsara and it is in fact an infinite cycle that ends in unity of spirit (Moksha). This is the ultimate escape from the process of rebirth. This process is under the rule of "Karma" that keeps a tally of the good and bad we have done in this life which will have a governing ramification on the next life.

❖ If you have not reached this Moksha, then you are still in a condition of disillusionment, searching along your many lives into the ultimate union or oneness of being.

Q8. Are All Religions the same Idea?

❖ In Hinduism there are four approaches to reconciliation the ultimate reality, Moksha
   • You can practise yoga in a process of attainment.
   • You can regularly serve and sacrifice to one of the many god's recognized by Hinduism.
   • You can perform regular pilgrimage to designated holy sites.
   • You can study and lean from several of the Holy Books and reach a great understanding of their teachings to advance through the Dharma the ritualistic observances contained in the Vedas

Q10. Are Humans unique or just another Species?

❖ Humans need to be diligent in their lives as they may impact others whose Karmic past have brought them into a different state of being such as a cow or lower caste individual. The difficulty in one person's life impacting upon another creature's life are matters of Karmic concern.

❖ So, humans are not necessarily seen as the pinnacle of all species. Your behaviour is more critical to your future. However, it is difficult to know what your karma outcomes are to be because there is very little consensus between the saying of one guru and another as is true also between the writings of the Vedas.

❖ In both cases, (Pantheistic & polytheism) there is the idea that there is a governing law of "Karma" that keeps a tally of the good and bad we have done in this life which will have a governing ramification on the next life. This also leads to a caste system that is allowed and celebrated, so as to keep each group enslaved to their current existence on the off chance that they will be better off in the next life. In both cases there is a strong belief in a new life being reborn into anything living, from earth-worn to a Brahmin caste man, the highest priestly caste. One wonder who thought that up…?

❖ Hindus believe that humanity and the Being of ultimate Oneness (Brahman) are separate but can be united though the infinite representations of gods and goddesses. These deities become incarnate within the idols, temples, gurus', rivers, animals and other beings or objects. Man is subject to the "Law of Karma" and he spends his time on earths as a result of his previous lives on earth in the circle of existence, trying to be reborn into the highest life form and thereby be ultimately united in Brahman.

❖ The goal of man, then is to work his way out of this life by the best possible performance, overcoming their own evil actions and progressing to better lives, until they are ultimately joined in "spiritual" oneness. They work out this earthly life and the cycle of Karma by:

  • Being lovingly devoted to any of the Hindu deities.
  • Growing in the knowledge through meditation of Brahmana spiritual oneness.
  • The soul of man is the only significant part of man because it is destined to be united with Brahman.
  • Realizing that circumstances in this life are not real and that selfhood is an illusion.

❖ This is accomplished by meditation and being dedicated to various religious ceremonies and rites as determined by the deities.

❖ Reality is in Braham because only Brahman is ultimately real.

❖ So, the purpose of man is to be united with Brahman when you achieve full recognition that personhood is the illusion to be overcome.

Buddhism:

Q1. Does God exist?

❖ Buddha taught that the world was an illusion and that the understanding of the future was to come into unity with their ideal "Nirvana". This a pantheistic belief that there exists an impersonal reality of infinite existence, so if we can just leave our finite self and join this impersonal reality(Nirvana), we will have union with the infinite. Nirvana is described as beyond being and beyond nonbeing. Their assessment of the afterlife is like Hinduism with the idea of reincarnation, only we progress as we learn the eight-fold paths of yoga, through mental techniques and physical exercises to facilitate our union with the infinite Oneness. So, no; the idea of God for Buddhism is not considered a question that can be answered.

Q2. What has God Said?

❖ Buddha speaks for any idea that is worthy of thought. He is seen as the ultimate holy man or guru who is to be followed in practices as outlined:

❖ Their idea of reincarnation is a mechanistic rule, that as we progress in this life along the road of achieving union with the impersonal reality we will cease to exist here and ultimately be one with everything which is described as "Nirvana". This is done by accepting the **"The Four Noble Truths"** that Buddha taught when he Turned the Wheel of Dharma. In order to understand Buddhism beliefs and practices, one must learn and then apply:

❖ **the Four Nobles**

- The First Noble Truth is: Suffering Exists. While suffering is realistic in life, it is because we do not understand why we suffer.
- The Second Noble Truth is The Cause of Suffering, which is our ignorance. So, we need to come to an understanding that mind and our attachments on earth are the cause of our suffering.
- The Third Noble Truth is the End Suffering is when we detach ourselves from desire or attachments here on earth and achieve what is termed Nirvana.
- The Fourth Noble Truth in the path to Freedom, is in practicing the Eight-Fold Path to enlightenment.

❖ **the Eight-Fold Path:**
  ○ **Right View**
  ○ **Right Thought**
  ○ **Right Speech**
  ○ **Right Action**
  ○ **Right Livelihood**
  ○ **Right Effort**
  ○ **Right Mindfulness**
  ○ **Right Concentration**

❖ The eight-fold path is the way to enlightenment. Enlightenment liberates you to escape suffering, which opens you up to the ultimate union with the cosmic oneness.

❖ This is the end of all successful lives according to Buddha.

Q3. What is God like?

❖ God as such is nonexistent.

Q4. Who is Jesus of Nazareth?

❖ Jesus is a good teacher but not god nor is he the way.

Q5. What does Jesus offer us Today?

❖ Nothing

Q6. What happens when you Die?

❖ When you die you are either caught in the mill of reincarnation or you enter into a place of union with the spirit of oneness-nirvana.

Q7. Why is there Evil in the World?

❖ There really is not evil in the world, it is just an illusion caused by our self-awareness, which needs to be divested to liberate us into Nirvana.

Q8. Are All Religions the same Idea?

❖ No Buddhism is the right path to Nirvana and all other paths lead you to deception.

Q9. How Can I be sure where I will spend Life after Death?

❖ Think right and be right will lead you to Nirvana.

Q10. Are Humans unique or just another Specie?

❖ Man is deceived in his natural state. The need in Buddhism is to free you from yourself.

❖ Buddhism rejects the idea of deities found in Hinduism. Buddha never claimed to be divine but he is viewed as the one teacher to have attained spiritual enlightenment therefore, ultimate freedom from the circle of life and death. Like Hinduism, Buddhists believe that man is material and spiritual but the material needs to be divested in the true freedom from the cycle of rebirth. Suffering is the result of your past lives and the goal is to purify your heart from the selfish cravings of this world. If you can escape your own selfish ways then you will be able to connect with the Oneness of Nirvana.

❖ Buddhists see man captured in our selfish desires. To escape this captivity man must achieve oneness by personal restraint of fasting and meditations. This leads to becoming free from the physical body's needs and desire. Meditation is the pathway to Nirvana that allows you to extinguish all the flames of desire.

New Age:

❖ New age spirituality is an outgrowth of Hinduism and Buddhism but it focuses upon individual growth in understanding. It says that we are the source of all-knowing and growth. We are on a discovery to find the Spiritual Consciousness that is the connection to the oneness of the cosmos.

ADDENDUM 3

Atheist

There is no life after death. In order for there be life after death, there must be a judge who will determine good from evil. The judge will balance and judge our performance against the scale of good and evil. As there is no judge there cannot really be any determination of good or evil. The atheist is the sole judge of himself and others around him. This leads naturally to the idea of relative order, which then assumes that political correctness is the determiner of right and wrong. Each one will then make his own way in the world, operating on his own value system.

However, anytime an individual makes a judgment about good and evil, he is determining it, based upon the idea that man is but a product of his own DNA and thoughts, which are function of his material brain. Therefore, there really cannot be any guilt or innocence because it is all a chemical reaction that is the prime determiner of how we behave. Can chemistry really be judged?

Q1. Does God exist?

- ❖ Atheists believe there is no God,
- ❖ Their assessment is based they say upon science and material.
- ❖ If you cannot measure it or see it, it does not exist.
- ❖ Therefore, God does not exist.

Q2. What has God Said?

❖ God who does not exist has nothing to say.

❖ The only truth is what can be determined to be in nature through measurement and physical determination. In effect for the atheist, science is the only God.

Q3. What is God like?

❖ Not relevant.

Q4. Who is Jesus of Nazareth?

❖ He was a good teacher of ideas.

❖ Generally, they accept some of His teaching such as the golden rule, but it is not fixed to anything other than personal freedom and reciprocity in society.

Q5. What does Jesus offer us Today?

❖ Some good ideas and some foolish ideas.

❖ They reject the idea that you need to be forgiven for anything.

Q6. What happens when you Die?

❖ Your existence is ended and the body decomposes.

Q7. Why is there Evil in the World?

❖ There is evil in the world because man has will and sometimes he transgresses cultural norms.

❖ However cultural norms are to be decided upon by any society based upon their need's wants and desires.

Q8. Are All Religions the same Idea?

❖ Yes, and they lead you into deception.

- Buddhism is the closest world religion that might fit with atheism in today's world. Most, if not all religions, are counter to man's determinism.

Q9. How Can I be sure where I will spend Life after Death?

- You can be sure that you will cease to exist and your body will decompose.
- You will be the sum total of the substance on your tombstone.
- Your only certainty is, that for a time, where you are buried or scattered, is where you will spend your death.

Q10. Are Humans unique or just another Species?

- Humans are the top of the food chain.
- They are the specie that has most evolved from their humble beginnings.
- They are evolved out of the great pool of evolutionary process. Nothing differentiated us from other species, other than our ability for rational thought and self-awareness.
- Some are more evolved that others.

NOTE:

Each section of the Addendum is from my own research over the years. These notes are how I read the various alternatives to Christianity and what makes them incompatible with it.

For further follow-up:
Website: big-questions.ca
Write: info@big-questions.ca

BIBLIOGRAPHY

<u>Come Let Us Reason</u>	Norman L. Geisler & Ronald M. Brooks; Baker Academics, Grand Rapids, MI.
<u>Counterfeit Gods</u>	Timothy Keller; Dutton, Penguin Group, New York, NY.
<u>Grand Central Questions</u>	Abdu Murray; Inter Varsity Press; Downers Grove, IL.
<u>Has God Spoken</u>	Hank Hanegraaff; Thomas Nelson, Nashville, TE.
<u>Hidden in Plain Sight</u>	Mark Buchanan; Thomas Nelson, Nashville, TE.
<u>I Don't Have Enough Faith to Be an Atheist</u>	Norman L. Geisler & Frank Turek; Crossway Books, Wheaton, IL.
<u>Name above All Name</u>	Alister Begg & Sinclair B. Ferguson; Crossway Books, Wheaton, IL.
<u>Signature in the Cell</u>	Stephen C. Meyer; Harper One, New York, NY.
<u>Stealing from God</u>	Frank Turek; NavPress, Colorado Springs, CO.
<u>The Case for Christ</u>	Lee Strobel; Zondervan Publishing, Grand Rapids, MI.
<u>The Attributes of God</u>	A.W. Pink; Baker Books, Grand Rapids, MI.
<u>The Dust of Death</u>	Os Guinness; Inter Varsity Press, Downers Grove, IL.
<u>The Reason for God</u>	Timothy Keller; Riverhead Books, Penguin Group, New York, NY.
<u>The Soil</u>	J.P. Moreland; Moody Publishers, Chicago, IL.
<u>The Holy Bible, (New International Version)</u>	Zondervan Publishing, Grand Rapids, MI.
<u>Union with Christ</u>	Robert Letham: P&R Publishing, Phillisburg, NJ.

BIBLICAL REFERENCES: PAGE (S)

Genesis	1:1 (45) 3, 24 (126) 26 (44 &150), 15-17 (62), 28-31 (47 & 62); 2:4 (45), 7 (124), 15-17 (126 & 127); 3:8-18 (136), 14-15 (63), 21-24 (60 & 137); 6:3 (58); 9:12-13 (60); 14:20 (45); 15:2 (45); 16:13 (45); 17:1 (45); 19:3-24 (24), 21-24; 21:33 (45); 22:14 (45).
Exodus	3:5 (49), 14 (30 & 44), 4-4:17; 3:13 (21); 8:10 (46); 9:14 (46); 15:11 (46 & 49), 26 (45); 17:15 (45); 19:3-24; 31:13 (45); 32:9-14 (37); 33:19 (48 & 57); 34:6,7 (58).
Leviticus	21:8 (49).
Numbers	14:18 (58); 23:19 (42).
Deuteronomy	4:7,8 (34); 6:4-5 (43); 7:7-10 (52); 18:15-19 (77); 32:4 (51), 39-41 (60).
Joshua	24:19 (49).
Judges	6:24 (45).
1 Samuel	1:3 (45); 15:29 (41); 16:7 (41)
2 Samuel	7:22 (46).
1 Kings	8:23 (46), 27 (35); 15:33-34 (25).
2 Kings	20 (16).
1 Chronicles	16:29 (49); 17:20 (46); 28:9 (41).
2 Chronicles	32:2-3 (16).
Job	37:16 (41); 42:2 (40)

Psalms	2:1-12 (60); 8:1-9 (152); 9:10 (30); 18:25-27 (38); 19:1-14 (60); 22:3 (49); 23:1 (45); 25:5-6 (48); 33:4-5 (48 & 51); 52:1 (47); 59:16 (56); 76:4-10 (60); 82:1, 6 (43); 86:15 (58); 89:35 (49); 90:2-4 (38 & 40); 93:2 (37); 96:4-5 (43), 9 (49); 100:5 (47); 102:12 (38), 25-27 (33 & 37); 103:6 (52), 8-17 (56 & 60); 107:8 (47 & 58); 115:3 (40); 118:1 (47); 119:68 (47); 136:9 (56); 139:1-4 (41), 7-13 (34 & 35), 9-12, 14 (47); 145:9, 15-16 (47), 25 (56).
Proverbs	9:10 (49).
Ecclesiastes	12:6,7 (156)
Isaiah	4:10 (41); 6:2 (50), 3 (49); 9:6-7 (43, 44 & 74), 37 (16); 11:6-9 (162); 13:9-13 (60); 40:13-14, 18, 25 (46); 41:4 (31); 42:9 (41); 43:10 (43); 44:6,8 (31 & 43), 7 (46), 22-23 (41 & 43), 24; 45:1 (17), 21 (50); 44:7 (41), 24 (44); 45:5-7 (43); 48:12 (31); 51:6 (37); 56:5, 9 (46); 66:1-2 (33 & 35).
Jeremiah	10:6,7 (46); 17:10 (41); 23:1 (45), 5-6 (76), 23-24 (34 & 35); 29:10 (18) 31:33 (53), 35 (44).
Ezekiel	1:26-28 (47); 33:11 (56 & 61); 48:25 (45).
Daniel	2:22 (41); 7:13-14 (17 & 73).
Micah	5:2-5 (75); 6:8 (48 & 50); 7:18 (46).
Nahum	1:3 (58), 17 (47).
Habakkuk	1:12-13 (49).
Zephaniah	3:5 (50).
Nehemiah	1:17-21 (58).
Zechariah	14:9 (43).
Malachi	2:6; 3:6 (37).
Matthew	1:22-23 (78); 3:13-17 (24); 7:21-23 (68); 8:25-27 (72); 10:28-29 (71 & 124); 11:28 (89); 12:36-38 (95); 16:26 (156); 17:1-13; 19:16-21 (138), 26 (40); 20:20-28 (26); 22:23-32 (157), 34-38 (131); 28:1-20 (71).
Mark	1:9-11 (24); 8:34-37 (139); 9:2-13 (24); 10:16-18 (47, 60 & 67), 27 (40), 42-45 (97); 11:15-18 (80); 13:31 (52); 16:1-20 (71); 18:27 (40).

Luke	1:1-3 (23), 27 (40); 2:14 (47); 3:21-23 (24); 4:32 (52); 5:19-26 (68); 6:1-5 (72), 37-38 (101), 46-49 (90); 7:11-17 (71), 43-58 (102); 8:49-56 (71); 9:10-17 (79), 28-36 (24); 16:19-32 (154); 18:27 (40); 22:66-71 (69); 24:1-49 (71).
John	1:1 (21), 1-14 (164), 11-13 (92 & 104), 16-18 (47 & 107), 28 (16), 29 (21), 41(21), 1:49 (21); 2:11-13 (16), 15-17 (33); 3:14-21 (52, 132 & 140); 4:24,26 (21), 42 (21); 5:2 (16), 5:17-18 (67 & 98), 19-27 (98 & 108), 26(30 & 31), 30 (52); 6:35 (21); 8:12 (21), 24-26 (21), 31-36 (93), 48-59 (21 & 81); 9:7 (16), 10:11-14(21), 10:10 (101), 14-18 (97), 22-33 (70), 32-36 (43); 11:18 (15), 25-27 (21 & 48); 12:47-50 (110); 13:18-19 (21); 14:1-14 (144 & 166), 7-11 (105), 15-21 (105 & 112), 22-26 (26), 25-27 (105), 27-28 (89 & 91); 15:1,5 (21), 9-17 (92 & 114); 16:23-28 (91), 28-32 (89); 17:6-12 (102), 17 (51); 18:19-24 (100); 20:28 (21); 20:1-21:25 (71).
Acts	2:22-33 (83); 3:14-21 (133 & 140); 6:1-7:59 (19), 7:48-49 (35), 54-56 (74); 9:3-6 (20); 11:6 (58); 13:46 (58);17:24-26 (36), 27 (34), 31 (50), 35 (56); 20:7 (20).
Romans	1:18-20 (30), 23 (37), 19-26 (58 & 95), 28-2:4 (60); 2:2 (52), 14 (60); 3:25-26 (119 & 142), 36 (50); 4:4 (57), 16 (58); 5:6-11 (53, 107 & 143), 12-15 (108); 8:26-30 (47 & 106), 35-39 (55); 9:15 (57), 22-24 (60); 10:9-10 (141); 13:8 (37) 11:6 (57).
1 Corinthians	6:2 (20), 8:4-6 (43); 10:20 (43); 13:1-13 (54).
2 Corinthians	1:21-23 (162); 3:1-8 (158); 4:4 (43).
Galatians	1:1-5 (86); 3:20 (43); 5:16-26 (113).
Ephesians	1:4-5 (53), 11 (40), 13-14 (104), 23 (36); 2:4-8 (57); 3:21 (38); 4:5-6 (43), 10 (36).
Philippians	4:19 (43).
Colossians	3:11 (36).
1 Thessalonians	2:4 (43).
2 Thessalonians	1:12 (57).
1 Timothy	2:5 (43); 5:21 (57).
2 Timothy	3:16-17 (52).

Hebrews	1:1,2 (39, 40, 44 & 47), 11-12 (37); 4:13-16 (41 & 100); 7:25-26 (85); 10:30-31 (61); 11:3 (39 & 40); 12:39 (50); 16:18 (51).
James	1:17 (37 & 55); 2:19 (43).
1 Peter	1:3-12 (84), 17-19 (50); 3:18 (103, 133 & 137), 20 (58).
2 Peter	1:12 (52); 2:4-11 (61); 3:8 (40), 9 (60).
1, John	1:2-4, (93), 5 (47, 49 & 60), 6-8 (94); 16-17 (55); 2:1-2 (141), 15-17; 4:7-21 (53).
Titus	1:1-3 (51); 2:11 (47 & 60); 3:5 (56).
Revelation	1:3,8 (31), 13-16 (47), 18 (31), 22 (28); 2:2 (52), 8 (31); 3:14 (31); 21:6 (31); 22:13 (31), 18-19.

Printed in the United States
by Baker & Taylor Publisher Services